ANIMALS GO TO WAR
FROM DOGS TO DOLPHINS

*This book is dedicated to the millions of animals that
have served humankind in war and in peace.*

Twenty-First Century Books
A division of Lerner Publishing Group, Inc.
241 First Avenue North
Minneapolis, MN 55401 USA

For reading levels and more information, look up this title at www.lernerbooks.com.

Main body text set in Adobe Garamond Pro 11/15.
Typeface provided by Adobe Systems.

Library of Congress Cataloging-in-Publication Data

Names: Goldsmith, Connie, 1945– author.
Title: Animals go to war : from dogs to dolphins / by Connie Goldsmith.
Description: Minneapolis, MN : Twenty-First Century Books, 2019. | Includes
    bibliographical references and index. | Audience: 13–18.
Identifiers: LCCN 2017060318 (print) | LCCN 2018000584 (ebook) |
    ISBN 9781541524804 (eb pdf) | ISBN 9781512498042 (lb : alk. paper)
Subjects: LCSH: Animals—War use—Juvenile literature. | Animals—War use—
    History—Juvenile literature.
Classification: LCC UH87 (ebook) | LCC UH87 .G65 2019 (print) |
    DDC 355.4/24—dc23

LC record available at https://lccn.loc.gov/2017060318

Manufactured in the United States of America
1-43531-33329-4/5/2018

ANIMALS GO TO WAR

FROM DOGS TO DOLPHINS

CONNIE GOLDSMITH

TWENTY-FIRST CENTURY BOOKS / MINNEAPOLIS

CONTENTS

CHAPTER 1

COMRADES IN WAR

JUDY AND FRANK

> One of the only good things about war was the love
> that grew between the soldiers and their animals. For
> a man far from home, frightened, alone, facing death,
> a horse, an ox, or even a ferret mascot, who could
> return affection, was an immeasurable comfort.
>
> —*Jilly Cooper,* Animals in War, *2006*

On June 26, 1944, toward the end of World War II (1939–1945), the Japanese ship *Harukiku Maru* was steaming through the Strait of Malacca between Malaysia and Indonesia. On its way to Singapore, the vessel held more than eleven hundred prisoners of war (POWs)—mostly British and Australian—jammed into its holds. A British submarine, not realizing the *Harukiku Maru* was carrying friendly Allied soldiers, fired two torpedoes into the ship, ripping it apart and blowing passengers into the turbulent water.

Prisoner of War # 81A was one of the lucky ones, escaping through a porthole just before the *Harukiku Maru* sank. The POW was a good swimmer and could have reached shore easily. Instead, # 81A rescued at least four drowning men by ferrying them to pieces of floating debris or rescue boats.

As exhaustion set in and POW # 81A could no longer swim, two other POWs lifted her from the sea. They hid her under a sail along with dead soldiers so none of the Japanese who looked into their boat

Judy the English pointer receives a Dickin Medal in London on May 2, 1946. On the right is Judy's owner, airman Frank Williams. He received the White Cross of St. Giles for bravery in saving an animal. Judy spent three and one-half years in Japanese prisoner-of-war camps and narrowly escaped death many times during the war.

would see her. "She was more dead than alive," one survivor recalled. "She had totally given herself to the drowning men."

Who was POW # 81A? Judy—a purebred English pointer.

GUNBOAT JUDY

Judy wasn't always a hero. In 1936, before the start of the war, she was a runaway pup from a breeding kennel in Shanghai, China. A girl named Lee Ming who worked at the kennels found the lost puppy in the busy streets of the city and took her back to the kennels. She called the puppy Shudi, which means "peaceful one" in Wu, the local Chinese dialect. The head of the kennel, who was British, called the puppy Judy. Wealthy British families in Shanghai adopted Judy's littermates. But Judy's fate would be very different from theirs.

When Judy was born, China controlled Shanghai, one of its most important cities. Shanghai had a large community of Americans, British, and other foreigners who lived and traded with the Chinese. Five years earlier, in 1931, Japan had taken over Manchuria, a part of China northeast of Shanghai. In 1932 the Japanese bombed Shanghai in a vicious attack hoping to gain more land. After a few weeks of fierce fighting between Japanese and Chinese forces, the League of Nations (a peacekeeping organization that preceded the United Nations) forced a treaty between the two countries. The agreement allowed only a few Japanese troops to remain in Shanghai along with the many international citizens and their military representatives. To protect against further Japanese aggression in Shanghai, the British kept part of its Royal Navy in China. It also maintained a fleet of small maneuverable gunboats on the Yangtze River, which flows into the East China Sea.

A few months after Lee Ming returned Judy to her kennels, two British sailors from the gunboat HMS *Gnat* visited the kennels looking for a ship mascot. When Charles Jeffery, the *Gnat*'s bosun (the person in charge of ship maintenance), whistled at Judy, she jumped into his arms. He took Judy back to the ship. "She is the most lovable creature," Jeffery wrote in his diary. "The ship's company love and treat Judy as a pet, and I am delighted that the men share her." By the next year, China and Japan were at war. The British were then neutral. But Japanese planes harassed and attacked the *Gnat* and other British gunboats on the Yangtze. Judy heard the planes and howled to warn her shipmates of incoming enemy aircraft.

With the threat of world war on the horizon, Judy and her human shipmates transferred to a bigger gunboat called the HMS *Grasshopper*. They steamed to Singapore, home to Britain's largest naval base in the Pacific region. Frank Williams, a member of the British Royal Air Force (RAF), arrived in Singapore in 1941. On December 7, 1941, the Japanese attacked the US naval base at Pearl Harbor, Hawaii. The day after the surprise attack, the United States declared war on Japan and officially entered World War II. Together, Britain, Australia, the United States, and other allies fought the Japanese in the Pacific. In Europe US troops joined Britain, France, and the Soviet Union (a union of republics that included Russia) to fight the armies of Adolf Hitler's Nazi Germany and other members of the Axis powers.

PRISONERS OF WAR

In Shanghai chaos reigned as the Japanese hunted down and bombed British boats in the South China Sea and on the Yangtze River. In February 1942, Williams and Judy were on separate gunboats about 40 miles (64 km) apart. The Japanese bombed and sank both boats. Williams and his crewmates escaped from their sunken boat, as did Judy and the crew of the *Grasshopper*. Judy set out with the *Grasshopper*'s crew through the jungles of Sumatra (an island in Indonesia), hoping to evade the Japanese. Judy survived a crocodile attack and chased off a tiger to help her friends. Williams and his crew escaped by truck and then by boat. He happened to spot Judy headed into the jungle and wondered what an English pointer was doing there.

Williams, Judy, and their crews could not escape the Japanese. The Chinese surrendered to the Japanese, and foreigners—especially members of foreign militaries—became prisoners of war in a temporary holding camp in Padang, Sumatra. Compared to what would come, Padang was a paradise. Williams, Judy, and the other POWs were there from March until June.

Then the Japanese military moved the POWs by truck convoys—with Judy hidden under rice sacks—to a second prison camp in another part of Sumatra 900 miles (1,448 km) away. In the camp, Judy learned to scurry for cover when guards approached. Days later, the Japanese moved them to a third camp by train, and again, the men hid Judy to keep her safe. Conditions were much worse in the new camp. Blistering heat. Malaria. Giant rats. Concrete floors for beds. Hard labor and near starvation. Judy lived on scraps the prisoners gave her and the occasional lizard or rat that she caught in the jungle.

As time went on, the men got hungrier, thinner, and sicker. One day after Judy had lost her best human friend to malaria, she approached Williams in a desperate search for food. Judy sat in front of him, almost at attention, as well-trained dogs will do. Williams tousled her ears and shared his meager rice ration with her. She looked into his eyes, gobbled the rice, and lay down at his feet. They became best friends for life.

In 1943 Williams convinced a slightly drunk prison commander to make Judy an official prisoner of war. Judy became Prisoner of War # 81A, the only animal ever named as a Japanese POW. The human prisoners labored hard every day in treacherous conditions to build bridges, lay railroad track, and to tear down abandoned buildings in Sumatra. There was never enough food. The men and Judy grew thinner and ever weaker. POWs died of malaria and starvation. The Japanese soldiers guarding the camp tried their best to kill Judy. How could a prisoner have a dog, especially a dog that growled at its captors? (A Japanese man had kicked Judy across the street when she was a puppy in Shanghai, and she never forgot it.) Often Williams would take a beating when the soldiers couldn't find Judy. She lived like a ghost, learning to hide in the camp or to scramble under the fence and flee into the jungle when Williams whistled to warn her away from the guards.

DEVOTED COMPANIONS

When orders came to move the prisoners by ship to yet another camp, Williams taught Judy to hang upside down without moving inside a burlap bag slung over his shoulder. He stood in the boiling sun for nearly two hours waiting to board the *Harukiku Maru*. Judy sensed the danger they were in and didn't even twitch. The Japanese stuffed the POWs (and, unknowingly, Judy) into dark, stinking holds, crammed in so tightly the men could hardly move. Twenty-four hours later, the British submarine HMS *Truculent* torpedoed the *Harukiku Maru*.

As the Japanese ship went down, Williams had pushed Judy through a tiny porthole before escaping himself. They made it to shore separately, with Judy rescuing at least four men along the way. The Japanese recaptured all the POWs and carted them off to yet another camp. Judy made it to the new camp too. A British POW recognized Judy and sneaked her onto a truck. Williams remembered, "When I entered the camp, a ragged dog jumped me from behind . . . flooring me." It was Judy. "She was covered in bunker oil and her old tired eyes were red."

One morning a year later, in August 1945, Judy woke Williams and the other men with loud barking. All the Japanese soldiers had given up their posts because Japan had surrendered to the United States. The POWs headed toward the sound of a truck with Judy leading the way with joyful barks. The British RAF Parachute Regiment marched into camp to liberate the emaciated prisoners. After a month's recovery in Singapore with Judy, Williams and his comrades were to return to England on a British ship. Rules forbade animals. But since Williams had smuggled Judy onto a Japanese ship, he figured, Why not onto a British one? So once again, she jumped into a burlap bag and boarded the ship hanging quietly from Williams's shoulder.

It wasn't long before the angry captain spotted Judy. Williams calmed him down by telling him about the lives Judy had saved. And he told him how long he and Judy had been together as devoted companions. Then the captain radioed ahead for permission for Judy to disembark. Upon landing in Liverpool, England, Williams led Judy down the gangplank. An official with the Ministry of Agriculture was there to take Judy into quarantine. For six months, she would be cared for and watched—like every dog that entered England—to make sure she was free of rabies.

JUDY WINS THE DICKIN MEDAL

Since 1943 the People's Dispensary for Sick Animals in Great Britain has awarded the Dickin Medal to animals that have served in war. Launched by animal welfare reformer Maria Dickin, the medal goes to animals, "in recognition of conspicuous gallantry or devotion to duty in saving human life while serving in military conflicts." Winners have included pigeons, dogs, horses, and a cat. The medal is the animal equivalent of the Victoria Cross, a medal awarded to deserving members of the British armed forces. The ribbon is green, brown, and sky blue, representing water, earth, and air to symbolize naval, land, and air forces.

While nearly all the animals that have received the award are from the United Kingdom, several are American animals. These include Lucca, an American dog that worked with the US Marine Corps for six years in the Iraq and Afghanistan wars of the early twenty-first century. She lost her leg in an explosion. Reckless, a mare that assisted US soldiers in the Korean War (1950–1953), is another American recipient of the medal. Judy received the Dickin Medal in 1946 "for magnificent courage and endurance in Japanese prison camps thus helping to maintain morale among her fellow prisoners, and for saving many lives through her intelligence and watchfulness." The Dickin Medal is the most prestigious award an animal can receive.

Like Judy, this Belgian Malinois—named Mali—received the prestigious Dickin Medal after his role in military operations in Afghanistan in 2012. The medal bears the words *Gallantry* and *We Also Serve*.

JUDY IN PEACE

Williams visited Judy often during her quarantine. He shared stories of her bravery with journalists, who published stories about her in magazines and newspapers. The headlines in one newspaper read, "Gunboat Judy Saved Lives—Wins a Medal and Life Pension." During the six months of quarantine, the story of Judy's incredible journey and heroic acts made her a national hero. After Judy's release from quarantine, she and Williams attended ceremonies in her honor, went on tours, marched in parades, and accepted awards for bravery. Williams and Judy visited the families of many POWs who had died in captivity during the war. He said, "The presence of Judy seemed a way to soften the essence of these sad times and brought some comfort with many families that had lived for months or years in uncertainty about the facts."

In 1948 Williams and Judy moved to what is now Tanzania, Africa, to work on a British government project to plant massive amounts of peanuts for food. Judy died in Africa in 1950 at the age of fourteen with Williams at her side. He wrapped Judy in his RAF jacket and buried her on a small hill near his hut. Williams lived for fifty-three more years after Judy died. He never owned another dog.

CHAPTER 2

ARMORED TANKS OF THE ANCIENT WORLD
ELEPHANTS

> **Pachyderms [elephants] are strong and intelligent, loyal and creative, in peace and war.**
>
> *—John M. Kistler, elephant expert, 2007*

Like Frank Williams and Judy, warriors have taken animals to the battlefield with them throughout history. Egyptian murals from six thousand years ago show soldiers unleashing dogs on enemies. People have ridden horses to war for about five thousand years. Pigeons carried vital messages for the Persians and Romans in ancient times. They were also couriers in more modern times, during World War I (1914–1918) and World War II.

Camels, donkeys, and mules have faithfully served as beasts of burden during wartime, hauling supplies and war material. Even elephants have participated in war, carrying armed soldiers and charging opponents, terrifying soldiers who had never seen such gigantic animals.

ELEPHANTS AND PEOPLE
Elephant biologist Richard Lair believes that humans and elephants first befriended one another roughly five thousand years ago—and

by accident. He suggests an orphaned calf theory in which an elephant calf, perhaps an orphan, wandered into a village somewhere in Asia. Kindhearted villagers fed the baby, gave her affection, and provided the social structure elephants need. Lair comments, "Young elephant calves have no instinctive fear of man and are well known for seeking out humans if bereft of [without] elephant society."

Most elephants are easily trained and managed by an experienced mahout (the elephant rider and caregiver), but they are not domesticated. However, elephants are often agreeable to working with people. According to Lair, "Even though elephants are wild, they are willing to make a working contract with us, one that is mutually satisfying." Elephant expert and author John Kistler says we should think of elephants as companions or hired labor. "Tame elephants . . . are only tame in the sense that they cooperate with their riders," he said. "In exchange for special foods and good scrubbing baths in the river, the elephant will do some work for the humans."

BANDOOLA IN BURMA

J. H. Williams was an elephant expert who worked in the jungles of western Burma (now Myanmar) for a British teak company. In 1942, when the Japanese invaded Burma, Williams joined a British Special Forces unit that specialized in guerrilla warfare. The Japanese had driven nearly all the British out of Burma by then. But Williams remained in Burma with a small unit of men, feeding intelligence to the British in India as part of a plan to regain control.

By 1944 the Japanese army was moving closer to Williams and his unit to seize land and elephants from the British. Williams knew that soon the British would have to evacuate thousands of people—civilians, workers, and British army dependents—through the dense Burmese jungle, over the mountains, and into India. The British had drafted elephants for this work. It was Williams's assignment to get people out of Burma and into India. He would also have to save as many elephants as possible. As well-trained beasts of burden, they were far too important to fall into Japanese hands.

More lavender than gray, with pink freckling on his ears and trunk, Bandoola was an Asian elephant in the prime of his working life. His mahout, Po Toke, had worked with the forty-six-year-old elephant ever since the mahout was fifteen years old. Po Toke and Bandoola trusted each other absolutely. The elephant had spent years hauling heavy teak logs out of the Burmese forest using his tusks and feet to push them over cliffs and into rivers below. From there, loggers would steer the teak to the sea, 1,000 miles (1,609 km) away. Teak—used in building ships—was the most valuable wood in the world. Bandoola had a new job: helping to get people out of the Burmese jungle before the Japanese arrived.

A writer for *National Geographic* magazine said that when Williams first met Bandoola and touched him that he "felt something pass between them, and that this elephant would know him better than any other human."

In April 1944, Williams's group was one of the very last British units and groups of civilians in Burma to flee the invading Japanese. His group consisted of forty-five elephants, four British officers, forty armed men, ninety elephant riders and caregivers, and sixty-four refugees, mostly the wives and children of the elephant riders. For days Williams and his workers hacked their way through dense forest as they headed to the 5,000-foot (1.5 km) mountain range that separated the jungles of Burma from the valleys of India and freedom. When the group reached the mountains, they faced a sheer sandstone wall at least 300 feet (91 m) high. Williams and his officers noticed a high ledge and rocks jutting out from the cliff. Could they turn the ledge and rocks into ladderlike steps? Could the elephants climb the ladder? Gunfire thudded in the distance as the Japanese closed in. Williams knew there was no turning back.

Williams asked Po Toke if Bandoola could climb the steep cliff above their jungle camp. "Bandoola will lead, and if he won't face it no other elephant will," Po Toke said. "He knows how to close his eye on the [edge of the cliff] and won't put his foot on anything that will give. If he should refuse halfway up he can back all the way down as he has eyes in his backside."

With Po Toke's words, Williams knew that his daring plan was a go. So he and his men spent two days cutting and digging elephant-foot-sized steps into the sandstone. The trail was barely 3 feet (0.9 m) wide in one section, with a sheer drop on the outside and nothing to break the fall.

On the day of the evacuation, Williams climbed the trail and stopped above the most dangerous spot. There he waited for the others to follow. The elephants would go first, coming after Bandoola one by one. The humans would go next. At the bottom of the path, Po Toke climbed onto Bandoola and gave him the command to go up. The elephant put his front feet on the first step. He stopped. He stood there for one full minute, testing to see if the step would hold his weight.

Bandoola waited two minutes more, then three minutes. Po Toke gave the elephant time to think and to reach a decision. Finally, after nine minutes, Bandoola began his ascent. Once he started, he climbed steadily and slowly, as if he knew the fate of the refugees and the other elephants rested on his broad back.

Williams later wrote that just when he wondered if they would ever appear, "Bandoola's head and tusks suddenly came around the corner below me. Then up came his hind quarters as though in a slow motion picture. The [mahout] was sitting on his head and, looking down, seemed to be directing the elephant where to place each of his feet." Williams moved ahead on the trail. "It was more than two hours before I saw Bandoola again, and then he was practically at the top and all danger of his slipping or refusing was over. My relief and excitement cannot be expressed in words."

It took the entire day for all the elephants and people to make the perilous climb. "I learned more about what elephants could . . . do in that one day than I had in twenty-four years," Williams said. "Po Toke's intuition had been perfectly right and I am certain that we should never have done it if we had led with any animal except Bandoola." Every person and animal with Williams crossed the mountain range safely into India. Williams led his group to a huge tea estate, where the Scottish manager welcomed them. A few days later, Bandoola rewarded himself in a pineapple grove, where he ate nine hundred pineapples.

TRAINING ELEPHANTS

Ancient peoples used elephants for transportation, building, logging, and other heavy tasks. We know this from artwork, such as a Mesopotamian clay plaque from 2000 BCE. (Mesopotamia included parts of present-day Greece, Bulgaria, and the Republic of Macedonia.) The plaque shows a man on an elephant's back holding onto a strap wrapped around the elephant's belly. War elephants appeared in Syria about 1500 BCE, and Indian Sanskrit texts suggest that war elephants often were used then. Nearly all war elephants were Asian elephants. They were used widely in the ancient world, including India, Thailand, China, Mesopotamia, and other countries in the Near East, Middle East, and even Europe.

In ancient warfare, thousands of soldiers fought in hand-to-hand battle with swords, spears, and arrows, often on foot or astride armored elephants. The elephants were used like modern tanks—to protect the riders and fight the enemy. Armies clashed frequently, often seeking to expand their territory, and they needed many elephants for battle. Yet elephants take twenty years to mature, and armies couldn't wait. So, instead, they captured adult elephants that lived in the wild and trained them.

Early methods for capturing an elephant were harsh. The first step was to dig pits in the ground and cover them with branches. Then hunters stampeded elephants toward the pits. Several animals always fell in and died or were badly injured. Those that survived were taken for training. Another method was to build a corral-like enclosure with a wide opening at one end that narrowed and led into a holding pen. Men used fire or loud noises to drive the elephants into the pens. Another way to capture a wild elephant was to use trained elephants called koonkies as decoys. The koonkie (usually a female) carried two or three men into a group of wild elephants. The wild elephants don't notice the men perched high on the koonkie's back. The men could quickly slip strong ropes around a wild elephant's feet and neck. Elephant expert John Kistler wrote, "Remarkably, wild elephants do not attack the men or the koonkies, although they could easily do so."

The hunters selected the elephants they wanted to keep: large males for war, females to carry heavy loads, and calves to form bonds with people for easy future training. Training a wild adult elephant began with breaking the animal's spirit so it would cooperate with people. The elephant were chained to a tree for weeks. People stayed out of its way. Occasionally someone threw food to it. "The animal becomes heartbroken and thin," J. H. Williams said. "Finally it realizes that it is in captivity for the rest of its days and, after the last heartbreaking struggle, will allow a man to sit on its head."

After the elephant had accepted humans, specialized training could begin. For elephants going to war, trainers would gradually familiarize the elephant with loud noises. These included shouts, the sound of arrows flying through the air and thunking into targets, the clash of swords and spears, and the beating of war drums. Trainers introduced skittish horses to elephants so they would become familiar with horses in battles. Elephants wore armor made from leather, metal plates, and heavy quilted fabric on their forehead and trunks to protect against arrows and spears. Some elephants wore iron or brass spikes on their tusks for charging the enemy.

MAHOUTS

It took a long time to train a successful war elephant. The relationship between animals and mahouts was critical and was built over many years. The mahout understood the flag and drum signals of the army's commander, which indicated what to do next. The mahout knew the idiosyncrasies of his elephant too. For example, flaming arrows might terrify his animal or perhaps it turned more slowly in one direction than in another. In ancient times as well as modern, the mahout is the elephant's protector. He assesses danger and makes the best decisions for both elephant and human. Patience, perseverance, and common sense are traits of the best mahouts.

In early historical battles, a mahout and one or two armed warriors carrying arrows and spears rode bareback on an elephant's back. The mahout sat on the animal's neck and controlled it with foot signals (using kicks and nudges to the back of the ears). Voice commands were useless because they couldn't be heard over the din of battle. The high position gave the mahouts a good view over the battlefield and an advantage over enemies on foot or on horses. Later cultures invented howdah towers, elaborate seats on the elephant's back in which the warriors rode.

Elephants were a big psychological advantage to their armies, especially when they fought against enemies who had never seen them before. War elephants helped in battles in many of the following ways:

- Horses feared the sight and smell of elephants. When confronted with elephants, horses often bolted and ran away, taking their riders along with them.
- Some elephants were trained to pick up enemy fighters with their trunks and lift them up to the warriors on their backs. While the captured soldier struggled, the men on the elephant's back killed him.
- Elephants were also trained to chase enemy soldiers who ran on foot. They gored the men with their tusks or crushed them by kneeling on them.
- Elephants stormed through enemy lines, deflecting and scattering the men. The sight of charging elephants was a terrifying sight.
- Elephants could serve as giant battering rams, knocking down defensive walls and forcing their way into a compound. They could pull up fences and posts with their trunks.
- Some elephants were trained to fight other elephants, using their heads, trunks, and tusks to wound enemy elephants in battle.

ALEXANDER: "A DANGER THAT MATCHES MY COURAGE"

An excellent strategist in both war and peace, Alexander the Great (356–323 BCE) is one of the most brilliant military leaders and powerful rulers of ancient time. He became king of Macedonia when he was about twenty, after the death of his father. During his reign, Alexander conquered Persia and Egypt. His kingdom stretched from the Mediterranean region eastward to the border of India and included what later became Turkey, Armenia, Syria, Iran, Iraq, and Saudi Arabia.

Alexander first saw war elephants in 331 BCE in a battle against King Darius III of Persia. Darius had positioned elephants alongside horse-drawn chariots filled with warriors. From a distance, Alexander noted the elephants' gleaming tusks covered with spikes. Alexander had heard of elephants but had never seen them, and he was uncertain about their abilities in battle. So instead of charging into battle right away as he usually did, Alexander retreated to camp to revise his strategy. While he consulted with his generals, the Persian army stood in the sun with their elephants all day. They stood all night too, waiting for Alexander. Hot, hungry, thirsty, and cranky, the elephants protested loudly, and Darius sent them home in the wee hours of the morning. When Alexander finally attacked the next day, he and his men easily won the battle with Darius.

Alexander decided to use elephants in future battles. A few years later, in 326 BCE, he and his army—including one hundred elephants—faced off against King Porus of Pauravas, in the Indian subcontinent. From across a river, Alexander saw that Porus had aligned two hundred elephants to block the shore on the other side. He also realized the river's current was too strong for his elephants to manage. This new challenge was so dazzling to Alexander that a companion heard him say, "I see at last a danger that matches my courage. It is at once with wild beasts and men of uncommon mettle [determination] that the contest now lies."

Under cover of darkness and the thunderous noise of a storm and a rising river, Alexander's men crossed the river, leaving their elephants behind. They attacked both sides of Porus's army at the same time in a military maneuver known as a pincher movement.

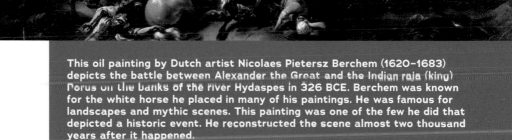

This oil painting by Dutch artist Nicolaes Pietersz Berchem (1620–1683) depicts the battle between Alexander the Great and the Indian raja (king) Porus on the banks of the river Hydaspes in 326 BCE. Berchem was known for the white horse he placed in many of his paintings. He was famous for landscapes and mythic scenes. This painting was one of the few he did that depicted a historic event. He reconstructed the scene almost two thousand years after it happened.

Alexander had fifteen thousand men, including one thousand archers on horses. He took about two-thirds of his army with him while he held the remaining one-third in reserve for a surprise attack. Porus's army numbered twenty-five thousand men and the elephants. Porus's elephants wore armor and carried archers and javelin throwers who fired from inside wooden howdahs. Porus himself, dressed in heavy armor, rode an elephant too.

Alexander's soldiers were the first Europeans to face war elephants in combat. The fight was brutal. The elephants stormed through Alexander's lines. The Roman historian Quintus Curtius Rufus of the first century CE later studied eyewitness accounts of the battle. He wrote that the elephants trampled men beneath their feet, crushing their armor and bones. "Upon others they inflicted a terrible death,

for they first lifted [the Macedonians] aloft with their trunks . . .
then dashed them down with great violence to the ground." The
Macedonians met the elephants' attack with equal violence, blinding
them with spears and crippling them by axing through their hamstrings
and trunks.

At the height of the battle, the rest of Alexander's army crossed
the river and surrounded Porus's army. Alexander's men had badly
wounded the remaining elephants, and they gave up fighting, as did
Porus's men. Although outnumbered, Alexander won the battle. He so
admired Porus's bravery that instead of killing him, as was the custom,
he allowed Porus to live. He also honored the king's elephant with
golden tusk rings. The ancient historian Plutarch (46–120 CE) wrote
that during the battle, Porus's elephant, "gave many singular proofs of
sagacity [wisdom] and of particular care for the king, whom as long
as he was strong and in a condition to fight, he defended with great
courage, repelling those who set upon him."

HANNIBAL AND HISTORY'S GREATEST AMBUSH

Hannibal was a general from Carthage (in what became Tunisia).
Like Alexander, he is considered by modern historians to be one of the
greatest military commanders of ancient times. Carthage battled the
Roman Empire for eighty years to control parts of southern Europe
(including what would become Spain and Italy) and North Africa in a
series of wars called the Punic Wars (264–146 BCE). Although Rome
ultimately won, Hannibal's invasion of the Italian peninsula during the
Second Punic War (218–201 BCE) is remembered as one of the most
brilliant military campaigns in history.

The armies of Carthage had proclaimed Hannibal as their leader
in 221 BCE when he was twenty-six years old. In 218 BCE, Hannibal
led his army, which numbered thirty-eight thousand infantry (foot
soldiers), eight thousand cavalry (men on horses), and thirty-eight
elephants, eastward through present-day Spain and southern France

While marching to Italy in the autumn of 218 BCE, the Carthaginian army under Hannibal fought an army of the Gallic Volcae tribe on the east bank of the Rhône River in southeastern France. This 1878 illustration by Henri Motte shows soldiers transporting elephants across the river. Historians aren't actually sure how the elephants got across the river, whether on rafts or by wading.

toward the Italian peninsula. From there he planned a surprise attack on the Roman Empire from the north. Some historians say that when Hannibal's army reached a broad river, the elephants refused to cross. Wild elephants are naturally good swimmers, but Hannibal's elephants were captured as calves and raised in Spain. They had no experience swimming. Hannibal's men built wooden rafts, covering them with dirt and leaves so the elephants would willingly board. Once the rafts were swirling in the current, the elephants panicked. Some historians believe that most jumped into the water and walked on the river's bottom, holding their trunks high above the surface to breathe.

To cross into the Italian peninsula, Hannibal's army had to cross the mighty Alps. They started their climb in mid-October that year. His elephants made the steep climb easily but slowly. Once above the tree line, where it is too cold for trees to grow, there was little food on the

PIGS AFIRE

The sound of squealing pigs frightened even the bravest elephant, according to Pliny the Elder, a Roman writer and philosopher of the first century CE. The later Roman writer Claudius Aelianus wrote that during a battle between the armies of the Romans and the Greeks in 275 BCE, the Romans dowsed pigs in flammable tar, set them afire, and drove them toward Greek elephants. In 266 BCE, during the siege of Megara (in Greece), the people of the city dipped a herd of pigs in oil, set them on fire, and drove them toward the advancing elephants. The shrill squeals of the dying pigs scattered the panicked elephants. Not only did they stop advancing on the Megarians, they trampled and killed their own men as they fled.

slopes for the elephants to eat. The animals became short of breath at the higher altitude. At the top, snow and ice made the trail slippery.

In the fifteen days it took to cross the Alps, the elephants grew thin and restless. Greek historian Polybius (ca. 200–118 BCE) later wrote that the elephants survived to fight only one battle against the Romans. Soon after the battle, all but one of the elephants died from wounds, hunger, or sickness. Surus—the surviving elephant—became Hannibal's personal mount. He carried Hannibal in a towered howdah on his back as the general led his men to a decisive victory against the Romans. Some historians called Hannibal and Surus's victory over a much larger army history's greatest ambush because an attack from the north across the Alps was so unexpected. While Hannibal won several battles during the Second Punic War, partly because of his surprise attack, he never defeated Rome. During the Third Punic War (149–146 BC), Rome conquered the Carthage Empire and became the most powerful state of the Western Mediterranean.

DIGNITY AND INTELLIGENCE:
TRAINING ELEPHANTS IN BURMA

Soldiers used elephants less often as time went on. Armies became familiar with the animals, less frightened of and more skilled at evading their attack. Horses also grew accustomed to elephants and were less likely to stampede at the sight of them. Elephants were fairly slow and prone to panic. When attacked by spears and javelins, elephants tended to back up or turn around and charge into their own army. So it seemed elephants were poorly suited for war, although they were still used occasionally in India, Southeast Asia, and China. The invention of firearms in the fourteenth century put a permanent end to war elephants.

Workers at a lumberyard in Rangoon, Burma, direct elephants as they move teak logs. This photo dates to 1908.

A US Army photographer captured this image around 1940 of an elephant loading supplies into a C-46 plane in India during World War II.

Even though elephants were no longer directly involved in war, people used them for other purposes. For example, they hauled heavy artillery and carried soldiers in Asia. In Burma the British ran an enormous teak empire during the nineteenth and twentieth centuries. Thousands of elephants such as Bandoola moved teak logs out of the forests and into the nearest rivers. Initially, British loggers captured and trained wild elephants. But calves born in captivity soon outnumbered them. Calves became friendly with their mother's mahouts from birth. Men and elephants live about the same length of time, so a young mahout and the calf he trained were together much of their lives.

By the early twentieth century, when Po Toke trained Bandoola, training was kinder and gentler than it had been in the past. Elephant expert and author J. H. Williams described how Burmese mahouts worked with calves. Training started when the animals were about five years old. A team of mahouts would lead a calf into a chute that was closed at one end. The mahouts tied the calf's legs with soft rawhide nooses to keep it from running away. The baby briefly struggled before quickly accepting the bananas the mahouts offered. Once the calf settled down, the team attached the calf's mahout to a pulley from which he hung just a few feet over the calf's head. The team would then lower the mahout onto his calf and haul him up, over and over. Soon the calf became accustomed to the weight of the rider on his back and accepted him there.

The next step was to teach the calf to lie down or sit on command. Another pulley held a heavy block of padded wood. The trainer lowered the weight for a few seconds onto the calf's back, forcing the animal down. The trainers called out *hmit*, the Burmese word instructing the elephant to lie down so the mahout could mount. To direct the calf to stand up, they called out the word *tah*. Mahouts could typically train a calf in about one day. When tamed, it would sit and stand up on command and tolerate a rider.

The mahout spent time with his calf every day to build a strong bond. He guided the elephant's movements by signaling instructions with body movements or with his feet, which he placed behind the animal's ears. The mahout moved his body, leaning left and right, for a turn, backward for halt, and forward for stoop or kneel. He dragged his foot along the elephant's neck, a signal to lift the right or left foot. During World War II, elephants in Asia hauled military equipment and pulled giant logs to rebuild bombed-out bridges and roads. Elephants carried food, bombs, grenades, large guns, ammunition, and other supplies. British field marshal William Slim said of the elephants he worked with in Burma during the war, "It was the elephant's dignity and intelligence that gained our real respect."

CHAPTER 3

LOYAL
AND TRUE
HORSES

**I would go to the horse lines each night to feed the
horses, and I would talk to my horse, and I'd talk
about my mother, and I'd talk about my sweetheart
and about home. And about being frightened. That
was all that kept me surviving.**

—*British World War I soldier to Michael Morpurgo,* War Horse, *2012*

I n 346 BCE, young Prince Alexander of Macedonia sat in an
audience that was gathered in an outdoor arena to see King Phillip's
new horse. Alexander's father had just purchased the magnificent
black stallion at a price three times the usual for a well-bred animal.
In the arena, the king's men couldn't mount the unruly horse. He
reared up and kicked at anyone who came near him. Disgusted, King
Phillip ordered his attendants to lead the horse away. According to
Greek historian Plutarch in his biography of Alexander, the prince
then called out a challenge. "What an excellent horse do they lose for
want of . . . boldness to manage him?"

King Phillip asked his son, "Do you reproach those who are older
than yourself, as if you were better able to manage him than they?"
Spectators laughed at the bold young prince. Alexander suggested
that if he failed to gentle him, he would pay his father for the horse.
Phillip agreed. Alexander approached the horse. He had noticed
something everyone else had failed to see—the horse was terrified

This statue of Alexander the Great astride his horse Bucephalus is on the waterfront in Thessaloniki, Greece. Alexander is a historic figure of mythic proportions, famous for having tamed the wild stallion.

of his own prancing shadow. Alexander took the reins in his hands and spoke soothingly to the animal. He turned the horse toward the sun so his shadow was behind him. When Alexander mounted the horse and rode the beautiful animal out of the arena, the crowd's laughter turned to cheers.

Alexander named the magnificent stallion Bucephalus. The two were inseparable. No one other than Alexander ever rode Bucephalus, according to Plutarch. As Alexander conquered much of the ancient world, the pair rode into every battle together. Enemy forces once kidnapped Bucephalus, and Alexander threatened such severe retribution that they returned the horse with a plea for mercy. Bucephalus died around 326 BCE, and historians consider him the most famous horse in history. Long before Bucephalus and long after him, horses have gone to war alongside human warriors.

HORSES GO TO WAR

Even though horses can be shy, high-strung, and easily alarmed, their speed, willingness to work, and loyalty made them valuable partners in war. Before domesticating horses for warfare, soldiers conducted war on foot with swords, spears, clubs, and bows and arrows. Battles were slow and bloody, and it was difficult for one group of warriors to surprise another or to escape when a battle was finished. Horses allowed armies to launch surprise attacks on their enemies and then to evade capture by quickly retreating.

Between four and five thousand years ago, horses transformed warfare, first by carrying armed men into battle on their backs and later by pulling warriors in wheeled chariots. About 1800 BCE, the nomadic Hyksos people of western Asia invented simple horse-drawn chariots and were among the first to use them in battle against Egypt. An army of racing chariots drawn by galloping horses with manes flying and carrying men shooting arrows inspired terror. But mighty Egyptian rulers were not to be outdone. Egyptians soon invented chariots big enough for three men: one man to drive the two horses that pulled the chariot, and two to shoot arrows and hurl spears. The chariot corps became the Egyptian army's elite fighting force.

Alexander's father put his army on horses about 400 BCE, the first European leader to do so. During the fifth century, the nomadic Huns of eastern Europe and Asia—mounted on small hardy horses accustomed to harsh living conditions—overran Roman armies. The Huns were superior riders, and their animals were tougher than Roman horses. And the Huns had invented saddles and stirrups. Prior to this era, riders rode bareback, clutching the horse's body with strong thigh muscles. Saddles provided for a more secure seating on the horse. Stirrups allowed Hun warriors to stand up and swing around in any direction as they rapidly fired their deadly arrows. Europeans quickly developed saddles and stirrups for their own horses.

On the south wall of the Temple of Beit el-Wali near Aswan, Egypt, pharaoh Ramesses II (1303–1213 BCE) is depicted in a war chariot charging into battle against the Nubians.

AMERICAN WARHORSES

American armies in both the Revolutionary War (1775–1783) and the Civil War (1861–1865) used horses. For example, during the Revolutionary War, Paul Revere rode a borrowed mare named Brown Beauty during his famous midnight ride from Boston to Lexington on April 18, 1775, to warn the American patriots that the British were coming. The Americans lost battles to the British and their experienced cavalry. So General George Washington, commander in chief of the American army and later the first president of the United States, wrote to Congress on December 11, 1776. "From the experience I have had in this campaign of the utility of Horse, I am convinced there is no carrying on the war without them [horses] and I would therefore recommend the establishment of one or more Cavalry Corps."

Cavalry units fought in battle during the Civil War. In this photograph from the era, members of Company 1 of the 6th Pennsylvania Cavalry Regiment take a break. They were known as Rush's Lancers for their use of lances (a long spear for cavalry soldiers) in battle. Artist Alfred Rodolph Waud (*seated center left*), Captain James Starr (*seated center*), and Lieutenant Frank H. Furness (*seated right*) are with the company.

Washington soon had his horsemen. The first American cavalry unit in the war was the Light Horse Troop of New York City. Mounted men moved quickly by horseback. While foot soldiers did most of the shooting, cavalry units patrolled, carried messages, monitored the coast for British landings, and moved weapons and supplies. In one daring raid, 260 American cavalrymen raided the British hay supply, stealing 300 tons (272 t) of hay and leaving the British with no way to feed their horses. Washington rode Blueskin, a white-gray stallion, into battles that helped the new country gain independence from Great Britain.

The Northern Union states and the Southern Confederate states used far more horses during the American Civil War than had been used in the Revolutionary War. When the war started, about 3.4 million horses lived in the North and about 1.7 million lived in the South. Horses were the backbone of the Civil War. They moved guns, pulled ambulances, and carried generals and messages. Horses were so important that General William T. Sherman, an important leader of the Union army, instructed his troops: "Every opportunity at a halt during a march should be taken advantage of to cut grass, wheat, or oats and extraordinary care be taken of the horses upon which everything depends."

Besides the work that horses performed, the sight of an officer on horseback rallying his troops improved morale. While Confederate soldiers often had to bring their own horses to the war, Union leaders provided high-quality horses to their troops. Many of these horses were Morgans, a uniquely American breed known for endurance, versatility, and courage. The largest cavalry battle between the North and South involved seventeen thousand horsemen on June 9, 1863, at Brandy Station, Virginia. The Confederate troops barely won this battle, but the success of the Union cavalry greatly encouraged the North. As the war went on, food shortages plagued the Confederate army and their horses. Many horses died during battles, but even more died from exhaustion and disease. An estimated one million horses (and mules) died in the Civil War, a carnage unmatched until horses faced the trenches of World War I in Europe.

WARHORSES IN WORLD WAR I: LOST IN THE MUD

The invention of the automobile in the early twentieth century radicalized transportation around the world. Americans and Europeans turned away from slow horse-drawn vehicles and bought new cars rather than new horses. Bicycles came into wide use. Farmers too began to adopt fuel-powered, mechanized equipment that no longer required horses and oxen for their power. As a result, horse farms bred far fewer horses.

World War I broke out in 1914 between the United Kingdom, France, and Russia—the Allies—and Germany and Austria-Hungary, the Central powers. World War I was a transition between older ways of war and newer, developing military technology. Both sides used horses. But mechanized and fuel-driven vehicles became increasingly important. Trucks, tanks, and cannons pulled by vehicles met horses carrying men, equipment, and supplies on the battlefield. The animals could go where vehicles could not, such as through mud, over trenches, on rough roads and, in some parts of the world, across roadless deserts and up mountains too steep for vehicles.

Despite mechanization, World War I armies all had horses. However, as civilians turned away from horses and toward vehicles, armies found themselves without enough horses to meet military needs. They scrambled to find solutions. In England, for example, the government quickly purchased or seized about 160,000 horses—workhorses, riding horses, and children's ponies—from British citizens. When that wasn't enough, the government purchased hundreds of thousands more from the United States, Canada, Argentina, India, and Australia.

Soon after the war started, the Allies and the Central powers were stalemated between treacherous trenches on the western front. This line of trenches and barbed wire stretched across most of western Europe and separated German-controlled land from land controlled by England and France. Soldiers faced each other across no-man's-land, a sea of mud, bomb craters, and charred tree stumps. "Nothing as far as the eye could see except waves rippling the mud as the wind blew," remembered Private Sydney Smith. "I had the terrible experience to witness three horses and six men disappear completely under the mud. It was a sight that will live forever in my memory."

By November 1917, the British were using an estimated one million horses and mules. The animals hauled food, ammunition, and supplies to the men in the trenches. Trucks couldn't make it through the mud or across the deep trenches dug into the earth. Often the horses couldn't make it either. If a heavily laden horse stumbled into a mud-filled pit, it had little chance of escaping, even with human help.

A World War I military convoy moves along rough terrain in the Dolomites of northeastern Italy. The photo was taken by Aldo Molinari (1885–1959) and was published in *L'Illustrazione Italiana* on September 26, 1915.

The surviving horses carried dead and wounded soldiers back to camp and then were led into their primitive holding pens behind the front lines. The horses grudgingly ate soggy oats served in wet nose bags because soldiers had little else to offer the animals. The Royal Society for the Prevention of Cruelty to Animals described the animals' conditions, saying, "Stables there are none. Cleaned [of dried mud] and fed [the animals] spend the night standing together in dejected groups, awaiting the time for a return to duty."

England's newly established Army Veterinary Corps provided expert care to injured horses. All the same, deaths among horses were high. More than one-quarter of a million horses perished on the western front alone. And, in fact, four times more horses died from hunger, illness, exposure to brutal weather conditions, injuries from barbed wire, poisonous gas, and broken legs than were killed by gunfire. Horses served in the cavalry in the war's global battlefields of

Egypt, Australia, Palestine, and South Africa too. They often shared a similar fate: huge losses due to starvation, thirst, and illness from exposure to extreme hot or cold weather.

Michael Morpurgo, a British writer, said that about one million horses went to World War I from Britain alone and that only a fraction of them survived. "Of those 65,000 [surviving horses], huge numbers never even got back to England because the government thought . . . 'They're not worth bringing back 'cause the price of horses [is] so low . . . we'll sell them to French butchers.' Having [survived] against terrible odds, and serving . . . the will of the soldiers . . . they then found themselves being sold off for meat." An estimated eight million horses died in World War I.

WARHORSES IN WORLD WAR II: STILL HELPING OUT

By the time World War II started in 1939, warhorses were no longer an important part of most militaries. But some countries still maintained a limited number of cavalry for patrol and reconnaissance. During the war, the Allied nations, including Britain, France, Australia, the Soviet Union, and the United States, fought the Axis nations, including Nazi Germany, Italy, and Japan. Nazi Germany and the Soviet Union maintained large cavalries and relied heavily on workhorses to move troops, artillery, and supplies. Horses seemed to be a cheap and reliable transport in muddy seasons. But they were expensive to feed, requiring up to 12 pounds (5.4 kg) of grain each day. Horses also required attendants to care for them, groom them, and to hitch and unhitch them to heavy artillery. And horses could only work about ten days before they weakened or got sick.

Germany had few natural oil resources to power tanks and trucks. So infantry and horse-drawn artillery formed much of the German army, especially on the battlefields of the Soviet Union. Germany

During World War II, Soviet army scouts patrolled rugged terrain on horseback. These scouts are in the northern Caucasus Mountains in 1942.

used about 2.75 million horses and mules in World War II, requiring thousands of men to care for them. As in World War I, many horses were lost to battle injuries, disease, and exposure. The Soviet Union lost much of its mechanized war equipment in a huge battle in 1941. In its place, the army formed temporary cavalry units. The Soviets had about 3.5 million horses during World War II. Because the Soviets had a good supply of oil and American supplies, they were able to return to tanks and mechanized vehicles by 1943. While Germany and the Soviet Union may not have provided accurate numbers about the number of horses that died, estimates suggest that the Germans lost 179,000 horses in December 1941 and January 1942 alone.

"GET THEM"—SAVING THE LIPIZZANERS

Trained at the Spanish Riding School of Vienna, Austria, Lipizzaners are world famous for their dressage (highly skilled and competitive style of training horse and rider). Dressage includes stylized jumps and balletlike movements. First bred in the sixteenth century, many of the snow-white and blue-black horses have been Olympic dressage champions and have appeared in live performances around the world.

Following an exhibition at St. Martin, Austria, in May 1945, Austrian colonel Alois Podhajsky (*on horseback*) formally requests that American military commander General George S. Patton (*standing*) protect the historic Viennese Spanish Riding School and its Lipizzaner horses.

During World War II, German dictator Adolf Hitler seized hundreds of Lipizzaners from Austria, Poland, Yugoslavia, and Italy. Obsessed with purity, he moved the prized horses to a farm in Czechoslovakia where he planned to breed genetically pure horses for Germany and to rebuild the horse-breeding industry in Poland.

The Lipizzaners' performance skills and beauty greatly impressed American general George S. Patton when he saw the horses in Austria for the first time as the war was ending. The Austrian in charge of the Lipizzaners, Colonel Alois Podhajsky, asked Patton to protect the few Lipizzaners he had left and to retrieve his breeding stock from Czechoslovakia. Patton agreed to do as Podhajsky asked.

The horses in Czechoslovakia were in imminent danger. Russia had received part of Czechoslovakia in the negotiations that were ending the war. The Russian army was quickly advancing to take control of their new territory. The Americans and Podhajsky feared the starving Russian troops would steal the horses or eat them. "Get them," Patton ordered. "Make it fast."

The Americans reached the horse farm before the Russians. American vehicles escorted a string of Lipizzaners, including pregnant mares and foals, to safety on a three-day, 130-mile-long (209 km) march. Colonel Charles Reed returned 244 Lipizzaners to Podhajsky. When asked about the dangerous mission that he had undertaken during the chaotic final days of the war, Reed said, "We were so tired of death and destruction, we wanted to do something beautiful."

RECKLESS IN KOREA

Kim Huk Moon called his horse Flame-of-the-Morning. The little sorrel mare was born in 1948 at a racetrack in Seoul, South Korea. Kim knew from the first that the mare was special. She was curious and smart and needed to be shown something only once or twice before knowing how to do it. On the day in 1950 when Flame was to run her first race, North Korea invaded South Korea. Kim hitched Flame to a cart and fled with his family.

Kim and Flame returned to Seoul in 1952 after the American military had driven back the North Korean advance. The track where Kim wanted to race Flame had been converted to an American airfield. Kim and Flame found work with the Americans hauling rice to a warehouse. In Kim's spare time, he took Flame to the partially demolished track at the airfield so she could run. American soldiers enjoyed watching the playful mare.

One day at the track, four US Marine Corps soldiers drove up in a jeep. They were looking for a strong, hardworking animal to carry the heavy ammunition for recoilless rifles. These guns were more like cannons than rifles. They each weighed about 114 pounds (52 kg), and their shells weighed more than 20 pounds (9 kg) each. The horse they chose would have to cross rice paddies and climb steep hills loaded with the ammunition. When Lieutenant Eric Pederson saw Flame, he knew she was the perfect horse for the job. Kim didn't want to sell her, but he couldn't say no to the offer. The money would be enough to buy his sister an artificial leg to replace the one she had lost to a land mine.

The marines called Flame Reckless, their nickname for the recoilless rifles. Sergeant Joseph Latham put Reckless through her very own hoof camp. She learned not to bolt at the sound and smell of gunfire. She learned how to hit the deck (lie down) under enemy fire. Latham taught her how to step over barbed wire and communication lines. On completing her training, she received the rank of private first class and the serial number H-1.

Reckless had her own bunker, yet she routinely walked into the men's tents for company. Horses are herd animals, and the marines became her herd. Her favorite food? Wheaties, graham crackers, and a helmet filled with beer or Coca-Cola, which she drank with the men before bed. Her intelligence and resourcefulness so impressed the Marine Corps that it promoted her to corporal.

US Marine Sergeant Joseph Latham trained Reckless during the Korean War (1950–1953). They pose together in this photo dating to 1952 or 1953.

During battles Reckless carried shells from the ammunition (ammo) dump behind the lines to the men on the front line and back again. She maneuvered narrow paths through boggy rice paddies spiked with land mines while firefights raged overhead. Between battles Reckless transported grenades, small arms ammo, rations, sleeping bags, and rolls of barbed wire. She helped the marines string communication lines from a spool on her back. "She could string more wire in a day than ten Marines and nobody could pack as much 75mm ammunition," journalist David Dempsey wrote.

AN AMERICAN HERO

Reckless is best known for her service during a particularly tough battle in March 1953 toward the end of the Korean War. For nearly three days and nights, she hauled ammo to the front line. She took breaks only for food, water, and short naps. Shrapnel hit her twice. Medics patched her up, and she went right back to work. One day she made fifty-one trips, carrying nearly 5 tons (4.5 t) of heavy shells under thunderous enemy fire.

"In all that intense fire, in the middle of that chaos, the image of that small, struggling horse—putting everything she had into it, struggling up that ridge loaded with 75 mm rounds . . . it was unbelievable," US marine Harold Wadley recalled." He compared Reckless to Bucephalus, Alexander the Great's horse. He said her sense of duty and determination surpassed his.

The war ended in a negotiated cease-fire later that year. By war's end, Reckless had been officially promoted to sergeant and she had received two purple hearts, a unit citation, service medals, and the Marine Corps good conduct medal. Yet it was her winning personality that soldiers remembered as much as her bravery. For example, Major General Randolph McCall Pate of the US Marines said of her, "She was constantly the center of attraction and was fully aware of her importance. If she failed to receive the attention she felt her due, she would deliberately walk into a group of Marines and . . . enter the conversation."

About a year after the war ended, in April 1954, the popular *Saturday Evening Post* magazine ran a story about her service in the war and wanted to know when she would be home. At this time, the US military did not bring war animals back home. Reckless was no exception. Because the military would not pay for the trip, a private donor paid her way. Reckless traveled by ship from Japan to San Francisco, California, suffering from seasickness all the way. Once she arrived in San Francisco, the Marine Corps held a reception for Reckless at the Marines' Memorial Club, where she entertained the audience by drinking bottles of Coca-Cola. Newspaper headlines across the nation shouted her name to celebrate her return.

Reckless spent the rest of her life at Camp Pendleton, a large Marine Corps base in Southern California. There she was promoted to staff sergeant. Reckless died in 1968 when she was almost twenty years old. In 1997 *Life Magazine* listed her as one of America's top one hundred heroes, the only animal ever to make the list. Reckless also posthumously received the prestigious Dickin Medal in 2016.

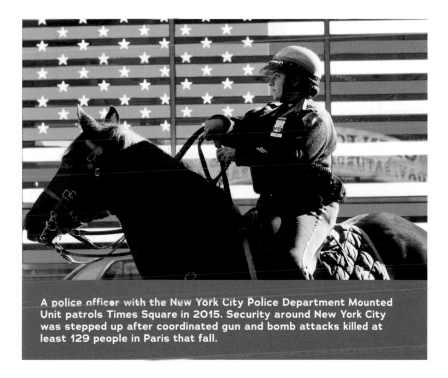

A police officer with the New York City Police Department Mounted Unit patrols Times Square in 2015. Security around New York City was stepped up after coordinated gun and bomb attacks killed at least 129 people in Paris that fall.

TWENTY-FIRST-CENTURY STATESIDE DUTIES

With the evolution of warfare technology, horses are no longer used in war. The military may include horses in funeral processions for fallen heroes, however. Usually twenty-first-century horses are trained for pleasure riding, racing, and other competitions.

Horses do serve in law enforcement. For example, many cities in the United States have police horse mounted units. New York City has had a mounted unit since 1858. The unit—with about fifty horses— handles counterterrorism, search and rescue, crowd control, traffic control, prevention of street crime, and community relations. "We can see far away and we can assess the situation by sitting on the horse," Sergeant Rafael Laskowski of New York's mounted unit said. "You can have 10 officers standing on the block, but everybody comes to us when they see us."

CHAPTER 4

BEASTS OF BURDEN
MULES AND CAMELS

> Having had experience of mules, donkeys, and horses, I would always choose a mule. I might not make a showy start, but I should still be going after everyone had stopped.
>
> —*R. J. Cox, British cavalry officer in World War II*

Italian explorer Marco Polo reported on and praised the Turkoman mules he saw in central Asia as early as 1294. Hundreds of years later, George Washington bred the first American mules at his home at Mount Vernon. He had received two valuable donkeys from King Charles of Spain in 1785 to breed with American mares. Historians credit the royal gift for the development of the American mule.

Humans have actually bred mules—a hybrid of a female horse and a male donkey—for at least five thousand years. In fact, many ancient peoples ranked the mule higher than the horse for usefulness and versatility. Egyptians relied on mules to pull chariots and to cart valuable turquoise across the desert to market. In ancient Greece and Rome, armies used mules to carry military equipment. And when Hannibal and his army crossed the Alps into the Italian peninsula in 218 BCE, he had mules as well as elephants with him.

Known for their ornery nature, mules often bond well with people. They are loyal and hardworking, and they show great stamina.

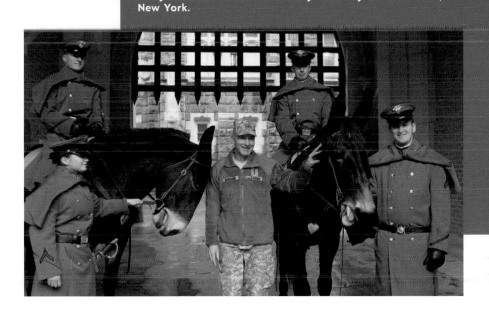

Two new mules were commissioned in 2015 as the official Army mascots at the US Military Academy at West Point, New York.

The mule has been the symbol of the US Army since 1899. The animals pulled wagons, and carried supplies and ammunition in several battles in the American Indian wars of the nineteenth century and in the Mexican-American War (1846–1848). During the Civil War, the Union army purchased one million mules to use as transport animals. "It was reported that President Lincoln, when reviewing Union army troops, paid more attention to the comfort of the mules than of his officers," Dave Babb of the American Mule Museum later wrote.

"A MOST SURPRISING ANIMAL"

"The mule always appears to me a most surprising animal," English naturalist Charles Darwin wrote in 1879. "That the offspring of the horse and the ass should possess more reason, memory, obstinacy, social affection, powers of muscular endurance, and length of life, than either of its parents, seems to indicate that art has here outdone nature." Military leaders of the twentieth century agreed and used mules extensively in World War I and World War II.

HERE'S YOUR MULE

This sheet music for a Civil War tune called "How Are You? John Morgan" dates to 1864. The song is about a Confederate (Southern) general named John Morgan who famously escaped from a Northern prison in 1863. The cover features a mule in reference to the popular Confederate catchphrases "Here's your mule" and "Where's my mule?"

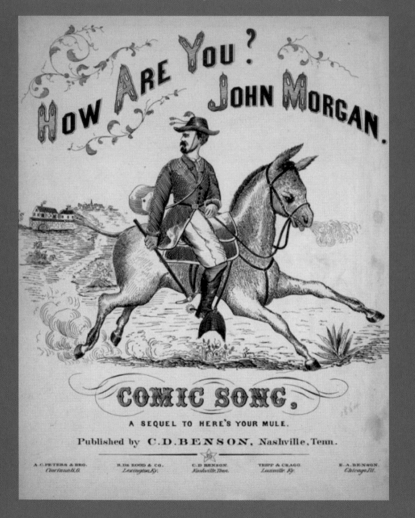

For example, Britain imported about 250,000 mules from North and South America during World War I to replace horses dying on the battlefields and in the trenches of the western front. Mules came down with mange—a serious skin infection caused by mites (tiny ticklike creatures related to spiders)—much less often than horses did. They also tolerated hunger and cold more easily. After a frosty night, even with ice silvering their big ears and blankets of snow covering their backs, mules endured.

During World War II, German and French armies used mules to pull guns and transport supplies on the battlefield. Mules served not only in Europe but also in Africa and Burma. Transporting mules by ship from Europe to far-off places such as Burma and Africa was challenging. Mules pretty much refused to be led onto a gangplank to board a ship. So soldiers netted them on the dock and hoisted them aboard. Once on the ship, the mules lived in hay-lined stalls. The voyages often lasted for a couple of weeks, and the mules were watered, fed, and groomed with great care while at sea.

The US military used at least four thousand mules in the campaigns in Sicily and mainland Italy from 1943 to 1945. Each fully loaded mule carried up to 200 pounds (91 kg) of ammo and supplies. Every day they trudged 20 miles (32 km) or more along steep mountain tracks that neither vehicles nor horses could navigate. The animals trekked as long as twelve hours each day for five days in a row, resting and eating only at night. Mules also served British and Indian Allied troops on the World War II battlefields of Sudan in northeastern Africa, where they worked even harder than in Europe. There, in stark desert and mountain terrains, the mules marched for fourteen hours a day, covering 35 miles (56 km) with full loads—water, food, ammo, mortars, machine guns, hot tea, and sometimes live sheep for Allied Indian troops, who favored mutton dishes.

British field marshal William Slim and his armies used mules extensively in Burma in World War II. Mules, as well as elephants

During World War I, soldiers used poison gas as a weapon. So men and military animals alike wore gas masks as a safeguard against the deadly gases. This photo of German soldiers and their mule dates to 1916.

such as Bandoola, helped evacuate Burmese and British citizens as the Japanese invaded that country. Mules presented a unique challenge in this situation. Instead of a hee-haw or a whinny, they make a loud sound known as a bray. Allied soldiers did not want to risk the mules giving away their location to the Japanese. So once the animals arrived in Burma, veterinary surgeons spread out tarpaulins in jungle clearings and cut the vocal cords of fifty-five hundred mules. When the mules recovered, they produced only a hoarse, wheezy sound.

Once, mules had to trek 200 miles (322 km) from the British airbase in Burma to reach the front line where the British were fighting the Japanese. It took too long and was too dangerous for the mules to trudge to the battlefield. Parachute experts developed a way to drop mules into the jungle in much the same way that jeeps and heavy artillery were parachuted. The animals were lashed onto wooden platforms and loaded into planes. Inflated pontoons surrounded the animals to protect them on landing. Parachutes were attached to the contraption, and once over their destination, pilots dropped the crates and the parachutes opened. When the mules landed and were unloaded, they were ready to work within minutes.

One exceptional mule in Burma was Mr. Bean. His job was to transport rolls of communication wire, which the British soldiers would lay out in the underbrush to carry messages. One day in 1944, while climbing a steep path, the men heard Japanese soldiers approaching. They dropped down the hillside, leaving Mr. Bean to face the enemy alone. Writer Jilly Cooper described it this way in her well-known book, *Animals in War*: "Surprised and pained to be so abandoned, he charged the [Japanese], kicking up his heels in a show of rage." When the men returned and reunited with the fearless mule the next day, they discovered he had been shot through his saddle and had broken ribs. But like most mules, he never complained and always endured!

THE WELL-TRAVELED MULE

The US military used mules during the Korean War in the mountainous terrain of Korea. The animals moved supplies where trucks and jeeps could not go. In 1951 a US Cavalry division captured a group of mules the North Koreans had abandoned after losing a battle. The captured mules were thin and sickly. The American soldiers fed them cereal and candy, and the mules quickly regained their health.

One of the captured mules had a US Army brand—O8KO. Army records showed the mule had served in Burma during World War II. At the end of that war, the Americans had given the mule to the Chinese Nationalist army. The Chinese Communists, who fought alongside the North Koreans, apparently had stolen O8KO from the Chinese Nationalists. After six years, the mule ended up back in the hands of the US Army, which promptly put him to work on a pack train. From Burma to China to North Korea, O8KO was a well-traveled mule.

This Assyrian relief from the Central Palace at Nimrud (near Mosul in northeastern Iraq) depicts captured camels. It dates to about 728 BCE.

CAMELS: SHIPS OF THE DESERT

Camels are perfectly suited for life in the desert. Long lashes protect their eyes from sand. Their nostril slits close during sandstorms, and they breathe instead through their split lip, which helps to keep sand from reaching their lungs. Most war camels are the single-humped dromedaries, although the Soviet Union used the less common two-humped Bactrian camels. The large humps for which camels are famous store fat they can live on when food is in short supply. They can drink huge amounts of water—25 gallons (95 L) or more at a time—so they can go five to six days without water. Thick coats protect camels against the desert heat. Their large, broad, and padded feet spread out their weight on top of the sand so they don't sink into it. Camels can walk up to 30 miles (48 km) a day for weeks while carrying loads that weigh as much as 450 pounds (204 kg). People have called camels ships of the desert for centuries.

Somalia and Saudi Arabia are probably where camels were first domesticated. The first known use of camel cavalries was in the Battle of Qarqar in 853 BCE in what is now Syria. In this conflict, the fierce Assyrian army battled a coalition of eleven kings, one of whom was the Arab king Gindibu. The king sent one thousand camels into battle. Not only did camels carry supplies, but many carried men armed with bows and arrows to fight horse-mounted men carrying the same weapons.

Armies also used camels to carry heavy loads, especially where horses and mules could not go. Later, in ancient Rome, armies took camel cavalry into combat because they knew that horses naturally fear the smell of camels, giving the Romans an advantage. If enemy horses came near the camels, they usually ran off. When Roman emperor Claudius invaded Britain in 43 CE, he brought elephants with him to terrify the Britons and camels to spook their chariot horses.

GOING UNTIL THEY DROPPED

European armies relied on camels in battle too. Camels aren't native to Europe. So when European armies went to war in the Middle East, Africa, and other desert terrains, they needed to acquire camels. Sometimes Europeans purchased the camels, stole them, or received them as gifts from local rulers. But when Europeans brought these desert animals into cold climates, the camels suffered greatly. For example, the British took pack animals such as camels, horses, mules, and oxen to work for them in the Crimean War (1853–1856). In this war between the Russian Empire and an alliance of western European nations including Britain, the British lost thirty thousand camels. Nearly all perished. Some couldn't survive the brutal winter cold, while others died from exhaustion and starvation. Russian general Mikhail Skobelev set out with twelve thousand camels to fight the Ottoman Turks in the Siege of Plevna (Bulgaria). When the battle ended in December 1877, only one camel remained.

In 1914 World War I broke out. At the time, many European countries owned or controlled colonies in parts of Africa and Asia. For example, German colonies in Africa included the countries of what are now Cameroon, Namibia, Rwanda, and Tanzania. French colonies in Africa included Algeria, Tunisia, and Morocco. Italian colonies in Africa included parts of Somalia and Libya, while British colonies included Egypt, Nigeria, and much of South Africa. The Turkish Ottoman Empire controlled much of eastern Europe and most of the Arabian Peninsula (including modern-day Saudi Arabia).

Battles in World War I between the Allies and the Central powers took place not only in Europe but also in Africa and Asia. Because so much of World War I occurred in Africa and the Middle East, the British created the Imperial Camel Corps (ICC) in 1916 for desert battles. The corps had more than four thousand camel-mounted soldiers, while another fifty thousand camels transported military supplies.

British soldiers at first resented riding camels instead of horses. However, as author Juliet Gardiner wrote, "The men came to admire their mounts [camels] for their remarkable powers of endurance and willingness to go until they dropped. The camels proved brave . . . under fire, even when suffering minor injuries and dripping blood."

Near the end of World War I, the British ran low on male camels. So the army drafted female camels. Though smaller and not as strong, females are calmer and more cooperative than males. Many of the females were pregnant and gave birth while on a march. "The animal-besotted British soldier was . . . very taken by these blond, silken-furred helpless little creatures (who looked like anthills on sticks) and refused to leave them behind," Jilly Cooper wrote. The men folded the babies up like picnic tables, placed them in nets, and hung them alongside their mothers' pack saddles. After traveling for a few hours, the men took the babies out of the nets for playtime and dinner. And the men learned to appreciate fresh camel milk instead of powdered milk in their afternoon tea. All told, the British lost 120,000 camels during the war.

LAWRENCE OF ARABIA AND THE IMPERIAL CAMEL CORPS

British officer Thomas Edward (T. E.) Lawrence, also called Lawrence of Arabia, was a legendary figure. He was an archaeologist, military officer, diplomat, and gifted writer in and about the Arabian Peninsula. He worked with the Imperial Camel Corps in World War I. Lawrence's role in the conflict was to help free Arabia (now Saudi Arabia) from the Ottomans.

In the spring of 1918, the corps was to be disbanded and most camels were to be given to the Indian cavalry. However, British leaders gave Lawrence four hundred of those camels and three hundred men to join with the Saudi forces. Their goal was to attack and destroy a vital railway that ran across the Hejaz region of Arabia. The railway was vital for carrying supplies.

Some of Lawrence's men ambushed trains and blew up railway tracks and bridges in nighttime sorties. Lawrence decided to use his camels to fool the Ottoman forces. He directed a few of his men to scatter empty food tins across the desert near their camp in Hejaz, far from the Ottoman's main front. The tins,

This undated photo of Lawrence of Arabia was taken in the Arabian desert toward the end of World War I. He was a legendary character and has been enshrined in film, television, theater, and even video games.

along with crisscrossing vehicle and camel tracks, would give the enemy the impression of large numbers of soldiers, jeeps, and animals. Lawrence's troops added piles of accumulated camel dung (used to start campfires) to the animals' usual droppings. The empty tins, numerous army forms filled with scribbling, and large amount of dung made it appear as if the entire corps and hundreds of men were in the area. The deception worked. The Ottomans stationed most of their men in the Hejaz area, severely weakening their main front.

Soldiers of the Indian Army Camel Corps ride down the Rajpath in Delhi, India, as part of the Republic Day Parade. Republic Day marks the date—January 26, 1950—on which the Constitution of India went into effect.

About three-quarters of the animals died from exhaustion and starvation, as well as war-related injuries.

The military used fewer camels in World War II, partly due to greatly improved mechanization of vehicles and widespread use of planes to carry men and supplies. Even so, soldiers in eastern Africa (in the present-day countries of Eritrea, Ethiopia, and Somaliland) used thousands of camels to transport men and supplies in the deserts and mountains. In August 1940, a small number of Somali camel cavalry fought off an invading Italian force of tanks and large artillery until reinforcements arrived to take up the battle. In 1943 some military units of the Soviet army in the southern part of the Soviet Union began using camels to transport ammunition, fuel, food, and even wounded Soviet soldiers. Primitive roads, steep terrain, lack of water, and a shortage of military vehicles in the Soviet armed forces made camels an important means of transport.

In the twenty-first century, camels no longer go to war. However, camel-mounted United Nations peacekeeping soldiers use camels in parts of Africa to patrol and monitor hot spots, such as border clashes between Eritrea and Ethiopia. Several Middle Eastern countries, such as Jordan, Oman, and Saudi Arabia, maintain camel corps for parades and ceremonies. Many rural peoples of the Middle East live with camels, which provide milk and meat to their families. Some people keep camels for pets. They race them, use them on camping trips, or enter them in camel beauty contests.

CHAPTER 5

FEATHERED HEROES
PIGEONS

When troops are lost or surrounded we depend absolutely on the pigeon for our communications. If it became necessary to discard every line and method of communications used on the front except one, I should unhesitatingly choose the pigeons.

—*General John Fowler, British Expeditionary Force, 1935*

Both revered and reviled—sometimes called rats with feathers—pigeons have been trusty messengers for human beings for about ten thousand years. They are speedy and dependable. They have a natural homing ability, always coming back to their home base after any flight, even when released from an unfamiliar location many miles away. Ancient Egyptians, for example, sent pigeons across their realm to announce the birth of new pharaohs. Ancient Greeks sent a pigeon from Olympia (the site of the Olympics) to Athens to spread the results of the world's first Olympic Games in 776 BCE. The great military leader Hannibal relied on pigeons to carry messages to his commanders in the battles they fought in the second century BCE. The ancient Roman army also used pigeons to carry military messages in their battles. Genghis Khan, founder of the great Mongol Empire in the thirteenth century CE, even created a pigeon postal service that spanned much of Asia and eastern Europe.

In more modern times, four hundred French pigeons carried thousands of government and military messages and about one million private messages during the Franco-Prussian War (1870–1871). During this five-month siege of Paris, the German army surrounded the city and cut off official channels of communication. So Parisians got creative. They used hot air balloons to carry baskets of homing pigeons and mail out of the city and into the countryside. People there would attach messages to the birds and release them to return to Paris. Pigeons allowed the French to stay in touch when other forms of communication failed. And by this time in history, the new process of microphotography had made it possible to reduce film images to a small size. In fact, one pigeon could carry thirty thousand messages on one roll of microfilm. In this way, pigeons and new technology helped European armies to share large amounts of information quickly.

During World War I and World War II, at least one million pigeons carried lifesaving messages. Pilots dropped pigeons strapped into parachutes from planes, and soldiers released them from armored tanks. Troops carried pigeons in baskets strapped to their chests.

Pigeons are one-way birds. Once they reached their destinations on the battlefield, commanders would write messages about how the battle was going and release the birds. The pigeons would immediately head back to their loft or pigeon coop at headquarters. As they flew, pigeons learned how to avoid snipers, machine gun fire, artillery shells, and poisonous gas. They evaded killer falcons, and flew through storms, across water, and over mountains. They flew on and on, even after losing an eye, a leg, or part of a wing.

Meet Cher Ami from World War I and Winkie from World War II. These two heroic pigeons saved lives and received medals for their military service.

CHER AMI SAVES THE LOST BATTALION

The British steamer rolled in the English Channel's choppy water on its way to France in the fall of 1918. Six hundred homing pigeons hunkered down in baskets lashed to the deck, lurching and rolling along with the ship. Heavy canvas covered the baskets to protect the pigeons from cold and fog. US general John Pershing had called for more pigeons in France to assist in the war against Germany. Armies used telephone and telegraph lines to communicate at the time, but the enemy all too frequently cut them. Pigeons were often more reliable than any other method of communication.

In response to Pershing's request, British pigeon breeders sent some of their best pigeons, including one named Cher Ami. Once in France, Cher Ami joined the US Army Pigeon Service (also called the US Army Signal Corps). He settled into his new home, a pigeon loft in the French city of Langres. A few days later, pigeon keepers moved Cher Ami and dozens of other pigeons into a mobile loft. A truck towed the loft to Rampont, a small village about 25 miles (40 km) from the Forest of Argonne. In the Argonne, the Allies and the

Cher Ami was one of about one million pigeons who served during World War I. Pigeons had various duties, including aerial survey work. In this World War I photo, a pigeon is outfitted with a small camera before flying its mission.

Germans were battling each other across a desolate landscape scarred by deep trenches gouged into the earth.

Within a few days, a British soldier hopped on his motorcycle with baskets of pigeons strapped to his body. He delivered Cher Ami and a few other pigeons to US major Charles Whittlesey on the front lines. The major was the leader of a battalion of soldiers in the 77th Infantry Division. Whittlesey had orders from General Pershing to seize the trenches that separated the part of France occupied by Germany from the part that was still free.

On October 2, 1918, Whittlesey and his men pushed forward into German-controlled land. Every few hours, they sent a pigeon with a note attached to its leg to the commander at Rampont to let him know where the battalion was and how the battle was going. American forces flanked Whittlesey's battalion on one side while French forces flanked his other side. Whittlesey's men—and their pigeons—moved forward so fast that they didn't realize the American and French soldiers had fallen behind because of heavy enemy fire.

TRAPPED!

German troops quickly surrounded the 77th, trapping Whittlesey and his 550 men in a small ravine. The Germans barraged the men with grenades and gunfire from all directions. Communications went down. Ammunition and food ran low. The Americans crawled to a nearby stream under sniper fire to get much-needed water.

By then Whittlesey had only three pigeons left. He sent two of them to his commander asking for help. The first message said, "Many wounded here whom we cannot evacuate." The second said, "Situation is cutting into our strength rapidly. Men are suffering from hunger and exposure. Cannot support be sent at once?" By October 4, Whittlesey and his men were in terrible shape. Even worse, Allied troops were firing on Whittlesey because they didn't know where he was. Desperate for support, Whittlesey decided to send his last pigeon—Cher Ami—for help. "We are along the road parallel 276.4. Our artillery is dropping a barrage directly on us. For heaven's sake, stop it."

Private Omer Richards placed the message in the capsule permanently attached to Cher Ami's leg and released the bird. Smoke filled the sky. Artillery shells, bullets, and shrapnel flew through the air. German rifles targeted the pigeon as he winged his way out of the ravine. They knew the bird must be carrying a message pinpointing the Americans' location. Slowly, Cher Ami gained altitude. Private Fred Evermann, trapped in the ravine with Whittlesey, later recalled, "A shell exploded directly below the bird, killing five of our men and stunning the pigeon so that it fluttered to the ground." As they watched the bird fall, the men lost all hope.

But unknown to Whittlesey, Cher Ami had managed to spread his wings as he fell and soon had climbed above the heavy gunfire. Despite severe wounds, the pigeon reached his loft in twenty-five minutes. Captain J. L. Carney, stationed at the loft, later remembered that "a crowd of . . . men were sitting around and discussing [Whittlesey's hopeless situation] when we heard the bell in the cote [loft] tinkle.

Tell-tale stains were on the entrance to the cote and we knew a wounded bird had come in."

The men found Cher Ami lying on his back, covered in blood. Shell fragments had taken out one eye, and a bullet had blasted a hole in his chest. The leg holding the message hung from the bird's body by a thread of tissue. The pigeoneer carefully removed the message and delivered it to the commanding officer.

Minutes later, the commanding officer ordered the French troops to stop shelling Whittlesey's position. And hours later, American planes braved artillery fire to drop supplies to the men in the ravine. But the food and ammunition missed the mark and fell into German hands. As news of the battalion's plight reached the world, an American newspaper coined the term the Lost Battalion. The name stuck.

On October 8, American troops were finally able to break through the German lines and deliver food and medical supplies to the Lost Battalion. Ambulances transported the wounded to battlefield medics, and chaplains arrived to bury the dead. Of the 550 men in the battalion, only 194 remained uninjured. They trudged back to headquarters.

Back at the loft, American medics worked hard to save Cher Ami. A soldier carved a tiny wooden leg to replace the one that had been shot off. But Cher Ami didn't need it. He learned to hop on one leg. When the bird recovered, he joined other American pigeons in Langres.

By November 1918, the war was over. Cher Ami made the journey back to the United States in an officer's cabin. The French awarded him the Croix de Guerre medal (a military decoration to recognize bravery). American newspapers and magazines wrote about Cher Ami's heroism and the men he'd saved. He was so popular that schoolchildren across the country knew the pigeon's name. After a whirlwind tour of several American cities, Cher Ami went to live in Fort Monmouth, New Jersey, as the mascot of the US Army Signal Corps. However, Cher Ami died of complications from his wounds a few months later. He is the most famous American war pigeon in history.

NEHU.40.NS.1 (WINKIE) IN THE WATER

Homing pigeon NEHU.40.NS.1 struggled to escape the shattered waterproof carrier meant to protect her from the North Sea. Oil coated her wings, and frigid water dripped from her feathers. She launched herself into the chilly dusk, circled a few times to get her bearings, and set off for her home loft 129 miles (208 km) away in Scotland.

The pigeon left behind the broken wreckage of a downed RAF bomber and its four-man crew. Earlier that day—February 23, 1942—enemy fire had hit the Beaufort bomber as it carried out a raid over Nazi-occupied Norway. The badly damaged plane couldn't reach its home base. The pilot barely had time to radio an SOS message before crashing into the icy North Sea on one of the coldest nights in history.

The bomber tore apart when the plane hit the water. The crew managed to scramble into a rubber dingy. The impact destroyed the plane's radio, and the crew's secret weapon—homing pigeon NEHU.40.NS.1—nearly drowned before freeing herself from her carrier. The men had no chance to attach a message to the pigeon's leg before she escaped.

Would rescuers find the men before they froze to death? After hearing the SOS, rescue planes and boats set off to search for the Beaufort, but there was little chance of locating the men in the vast North Sea between Norway and Scotland. After searching 100,000 square miles (259,000 sq. km) of sea, the RAF called off rescue attempts. Hope dimmed at the bomber base near Dundee, Scotland, where the four crew members and the pigeon's loft were stationed.

WINKIE'S FLIGHT

Meanwhile, the pigeon flew on and on. Like most birds, pigeons don't see well at night so they hate to fly in the dark. And flying over a large, unknown body of water is frightening. Yet this pigeon flew across the sea, through the night, and into the chilly dawn. In good weather, during the daytime, the pigeon's journey would have taken three to

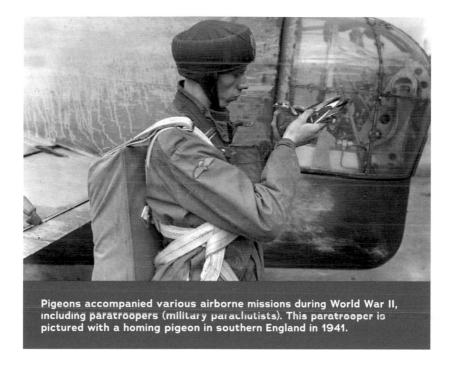

Pigeons accompanied various airborne missions during World War II, including paratroopers (military parachutists). This paratrooper is pictured with a homing pigeon in southern England in 1941.

four hours. That night, in treacherous conditions, pigeon NEHU.40. NS.1 flew for sixteen hours without stopping.

Shortly after dawn, she fluttered wearily into her home loft in Dundee, shivering with cold and exhaustion. Sergeant Davidson of the RAF Pigeon Service picked up the pigeon and checked her message capsule. It was empty. But because he could identify the bird from her permanent identification tag, he knew she was the pigeon assigned to the downed bomber. Using the Beaufort's last reported position, the strength of the wind and its direction, and the extent to which the oiled feathers would have slowed the pigeon's flight, Davidson was able to figure out where the Beaufort was.

The sergeant phoned his superior officer. "Sir, sir, it's the bird from the crashed plane. We're searching in the wrong place! That plane's come down much nearer Scotland than we think." With that new information, a plane quickly located the wreckage and called for a rescue boat. It took only fifteen minutes for the boat to reach the desperate men crouched in their rubber dingy. All survived, thanks to the plucky little pigeon that never gave up.

A few days later, the Beaufort's crew held a celebratory dinner in the pigeon's honor. Admiring officers offered toasts to her. The pilot praised her bravery. But she wasn't interested in being the guest of honor. Instead, she preened her feathers and nibbled at dried peas as she rested in her cage on the dinner table. Until then she'd been known only as pigeon NEHU.40.NS.1. That night the men christened her Winkie for her twitchy eyelid. (They didn't realize that her droopy, twitchy eyelid actually resulted from stress and exhaustion.)

Winkie's heroic flight was the first lifesaving rescue of World War II attributed to a pigeon. She received the Dickin Medal in 1943 for bravery in war. "I find it very, very moving really," British veterinarian Elaine

BUILT TO FLY

How could Winkie fly for sixteen hours? Pigeons are the perfect flying machines. They're built for rapid, long-distance flights. Exceptionally strong muscles power their large wings. Their skeletons are much lighter than other birds of similar size. In fact, some of the pigeon's wing bones are hollow. And their wings and shoulder bones work together for rapid flight. The wing moves in an arc from above the shoulder to below the chest, displacing massive amounts of air with each stroke. Even pigeon lungs are designed for long-distance flight. They absorb far more oxygen with each breath than do human lungs. Large amounts of oxygen provide the birds with plenty of energy for strenuous flying.

No human runner can match a pigeon's endurance. No cheetah can maintain a pigeon's speed. However, long flights take their toll. When pigeons complete a very difficult long flight such as Winkie's, they can lose up to one-fifth of their body weight. That's like a 100-pound (45 kg) kid losing 20 pounds (9 kg) during a soccer game. It takes considerable time for a pigeon to recover from a strenuous flight. Rest and good food are essential.

Pendlebury said in a newspaper interview seventy years later. "These people would have died without this pigeon 'message' coming through."

TRAINING PIGEONS

How did Cher Ami and Winkie come to be such heroes? Did they come by their skills naturally? Well, almost. Pigeons will nearly always return to their loft no matter how far they are from home, but they do need some training. A pigeon is ready for training when it is just weeks old. Training consists of putting the young bird in a carrier and releasing it at increasingly longer distances from its loft: a quarter mile (0.4 km) one day, then a half mile (0.8 km), and so on. Pigeons are social birds. The comfort of being back in their home loft is the only reward they need—that and getting their next meal of tasty grain.

Wartime pigeon messengers also had to learn to find a mobile loft—pigeon cages mounted on the back of a wagon or truck. Pigeoneers painted patterns on the mobile lofts, making it easier for the pigeons to find it. In wartime these vehicles moved frequently to follow the battle and provide fresh pigeons for the soldiers to use when sending messages.

Trainers took chicks from the nest when they were about four weeks old and placed them in their new home in the mobile loft. For the next two to three weeks, drivers moved the loft daily. The young birds took short flights morning, noon, and evening for several days so they could memorize their aerial bearings. When they got a little older, trainers would take them 50 miles (80 km) or farther from the loft. The pigeons quickly learned to find their new loft, even when it had moved.

Trainers knew a few tricks to push pigeons to fly faster. They would withhold food from the pigeon until it returned to the loft. Hunger was a powerful motivator, but jealousy was even stronger. Pigeons mate for life and are eager to return to the loft where their mates are waiting. Sometimes trainers introduced a new male pigeon to the loft shortly before releasing the resident male of a mated pair. When the resident male pigeon saw that his mate was with another male, he was certain to fly home as fast as he possibly could.

The military no longer needs pigeons to carry important messages, but millions of people around the world engage in modern-day pigeon racing. Top racers have flown 1,000 miles (1,609 km). Pigeons can fly 50 miles (80 km) an hour for moderate distances and up to 90 miles (140 km) an hour or more in short races. Other people simply raise pigeons for company and enjoy them for their charming personalities.

HOMING AND VISION

Many species of birds migrate long distances, with older birds showing younger ones the route. But pigeons don't migrate. They only know the way back to their home lofts—from pretty much anywhere. Experts have conducted experiments for decades to discover how pigeons home. No one has the complete answer. Scientists and pigeon experts do have theories. Pigeons may be able to see ultraviolet and infrared light, which humans can't detect with their eyes. They may use the position of the sun or have an internal clock. The birds may have magnetic sensors that pick up Earth's magnetic fields. And they certainly have extraordinary eyesight.

Charles Walcott was a professor and director of the Cornell Lab of Ornithology (the study of birds) in Ithaca, New York. Walcott studied homing pigeons from 1962 until the early 1980s. He and his team tracked hundreds of pigeons to which they had attached small radio transmitters. The team masked some pigeons' eyes with frosted lenses and covered the ears of other pigeons with plugs. Most found their way back to their home loft at Cornell. The tests suggested pigeons didn't need to see or hear to home.

Yet another study from England's Oxford University in 2004—published after ten years of research—suggests that pigeons need to see. From this study, it appears that the birds follow roads, buildings, and other structures to find their way home. But how do pigeons return home from unfamiliar locations? "For birds doing a journey for

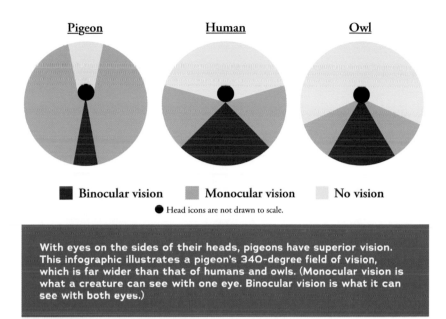

| Pigeon | Human | Owl |

Binocular vision **Monocular vision** **No vision**

● Head icons are not drawn to scale.

With eyes on the sides of their heads, pigeons have superior vision. This infographic illustrates a pigeon's 340-degree field of vision, which is far wider than that of humans and owls. (Monocular vision is what a creature can see with one eye. Binocular vision is what it can see with both eyes.)

the first time, they will use their inbuilt compasses and take sun and star bearings," Tim Guilford, professor of animal behavior at Oxford's Department of Zoology, said. "But once homing pigeons have flown a journey more than once, they home in on a [familiar] route . . . much as we do when we are driving or walking home from work."

Pigeon vision is far better than that of people and most other birds. People do have better binocular vision (seeing with both eyes). But pigeons have an extremely wide visual field—the entire area, including peripheral vision, that a creature can see when the eyes are looking forward. For comparison, the human visual field is 180 degrees while the pigeon can see 340 degrees around itself. (A full circle is 360 degrees.) That's a plus when danger in the bird's environment can sneak up from any direction. For example, pigeons can easily see the difference between a hawk and a vulture circling overhead. Vultures don't target pigeons, but hawks do. So a pigeon will immediately take evasive action when it sees a hawk. Pigeons also have better color vision than most animals on Earth. When tested in a lab, pigeons can see millions of different hues.

BIRD BRAINS

A number of studies at a variety of universities and laboratories in the last thirty years have shown that pigeons demonstrate behaviors that suggest they are among the very smartest of birds. For example, pigeons have learned the difference between works of art, recognized themselves in videos, passed the mirror test, and learned to distinguish letters and words on a computer touch screen.

In 1995 Japanese researcher Dr. Shigeru Watanabe of Tokyo's Keio University and his team trained pigeons to tell the difference between paintings by Picasso and Monet. If a pigeon pecked at a reproduction of a particular Picasso painting, it earned a food reward. If it pecked at a reproduction of a Monet painting, the bird earned no reward. The pigeons stopped pecking at the Monet reproduction. Then the researchers showed pigeons pictures of other paintings by the two artists that they had not seen before. They pecked only at the Picasso reproductions. This ability to tell the difference between the artists' styles compares to that of human college students.

In 2008 Watanabe trained pigeons to recognize themselves on live videotape. Pigeons were able to identify video images of themselves, even with a few seconds delay. This showed self-awareness abilities higher than that of three-year-old children.

One way scientists measure animal intelligence is by noting whether the animal can recognize itself in a mirror. Researchers place a mark, such as a removable dot or spot of color, on the animal's body that it cannot see. If the animal notices the mark when placed in front of a mirror and investigates it, the animal is showing self-awareness, a sign of intelligence. In 2014 Watanabe confirmed that pigeons do indeed display self-awareness. Pigeons, great apes, dolphins, orcas, elephants, and magpies are the only animals known so far to have this ability.

YELLOW   BLUE   RED   GREEN

Researchers have studied bird intelligence for decades. In this 1950 test, a pigeon correctly taps at the word sign that correlates to a particular color it is shown.

National Public Radio reported on a New Zealand study in 2016 in which researchers trained four pigeons to recognize dozens of words with about 70 percent accuracy. The smartest pigeon learned about sixty words that it could distinguish from about one thousand letters that made up nonsense words. Before that, scientists thought that only humans or primates could recognize letters. This finding might give scientists some insight into human brain development.

Jonathan Hagstrum, a geophysicist with the US Geological Survey, holds a very different view of pigeon navigation. During a 2013 public radio interview, Hagstrum reported on the way pigeons may use infrasound, sound too low for humans to hear, for navigation. Water waves in the deep ocean constantly produce acoustic energy (sound waves). "And that acoustic energy travels through the Earth as seismic energy, and then is reradiated at the landscape back into the atmosphere," Hagstrum said. "And I think pigeons and other birds probably are listening to that reradiated infrasound, and using that to find their way home." He believes pigeons use infrasound together with the position of the sun and Earth's magnetic field to navigate their way home. Some scientists believe that elephants, whales, and a few other large animals also probably communicate with infrasound.

If pigeons can't fly home, they may walk. A pigeon named Clarence didn't return home after a training flight at Fort Meade, Maryland, in the 1940s. The next day, a soldier found Clarence walking home on a country road. The pigeon had fallen into a pool of oil, and his feathers were so thickly covered that he couldn't fly. So he made his way home on foot! Whether it is speed, endurance, memory, or vision, pigeons have it all and will find their way home.

"THE GREAT WHITE SHARK OF THE SKY"

Pigeons aren't the only birds that have served in war. Canaries were vital in World War I. Because this species is very sensitive to the air it breathes, soldiers used them in World War I to detect and warn of incoming poisonous gas. Normally, the canaries sang, but they would fall silent or die when poisonous gas was present.

For this war, the British came up with a plan for smearing submarine periscopes with food. The idea was that when a German U-boat (submarine) raised its periscope above water to look around, gulls would go to the sub for the food. British soldiers on watch would

Peregrine falcons are the most common type of bird that airports and airfields use to ward off birds that risk flying into airplane engines.

detect the birds gathering around the sub's location and take it out with a torpedo. However, gulls aren't open-water birds. They prefer the shoreline, so this method didn't work.

Both the British and the Germans used falcons during World War I and World War II. They trained falcons to take down message-carrying pigeons. Pigeons can often evade falcons. But if the falcon stoops or dives from above, it has a good chance of catching a pigeon in its powerful talons.

Airports and airfields also rely on falcons to keep runways clear of birds so they don't fly into airplane engines and bring down the plane. This method of keeping planes safe from birds began in World War II. In the twenty-first century, some airports still use falcons to scare geese and gulls away from runways. "Falcons are the great white shark of the sky," says Mark Adam, who trains falcons to protect planes. "Birds are terrified of them."

CHAPTER 6

MAN'S BEST FRIEND
DOGS

The friendship of a dog is precious. It becomes even more so when one is so far removed from home as we are in Africa. I have a Scottie . . . he is the "one person" to whom I can talk without the conversation coming back to the war.

—Dwight D. Eisenhower, five-star general and later president of the United States, 1943

Who can resist love and loyalty wrapped up with a wagging tail and toothy grin? Nearly half the households in the United States own at least one dog, and many families own two or more. People who live with dogs know how deep the human-dog bond goes.

But how did dogs become such an important part of our lives? Did ancient humans tame cute wolf pups they had found? That's been the common assumption for years. Yet two scientists associated with Duke University in North Carolina have another theory. "Most likely, it was wolves that approached us, not the other way around, probably while they were scavenging around garbage dumps on the edge of human settlements," Dr. Brian Hare and Dr. Vanessa Woods wrote in a 2013 article for *National Geographic*.

DOGS HAVE IT ALL

Dogs make the perfect battle companion. Not only are they loyal and dependable, but they also have unique skills. A dog's sense of smell

is extraordinary. "Let's suppose [a dog's sense of smell is] just 10,000 times better [than a human's sense of smell]," said James Walker, a scientist who has researched the canine sense of smell. "If you make the analogy to vision, what you and I can see at a third of a mile [0.5 km], a dog could see more than 3,000 miles [4,828 km] away and still see as well." Another dog scientist said a dog can smell one rotten apple hidden in the middle of two million barrels of good apples.

Dogs can also hear high-frequency sounds that people can't hear, such as the sound of wind passing over the trip wires that trigger bombs and booby traps. Dogs can hear sounds about four times farther away than people can hear. And those movable ears allow dogs to locate and focus on specific sounds, even when the sounds are coming from different directions. While dogs don't see as well as people in the daytime, they have better night vision. And because their eyes are on the sides of their heads, dogs have a far wider field of vision than people do. With four legs, dogs also run much faster than people. These characteristics, combined with dogs' innate desire to please, make them the perfect animals to work with soldiers.

DOGS AT WAR

Dogs and humans have a long history together as military teammates. For example, Egyptian murals from 4000 BCE show soldiers turning dogs loose on enemies. Ancient Greek and Roman wall paintings of later centuries record the exploits of war dogs wearing spiked collars, chain mail armor, and padded jackets. When Roman general Julius Caesar invaded Britain in 55 BCE, his troops faced fearsome Celtic mastiffs, large dogs trained to fight in battles. Hundreds of years later, in the fifth century CE, Attila the Hun used war dogs against the armies of the Roman Empire. William the Conqueror, king of England in the eleventh century, also took dogs (said to be the ancestors of bloodhounds) into battle against his European enemies. The sight of large vicious dogs running toward a group of fighters on foot or on horseback startled and frightened both men and horses because the dogs had been trained to attack horses and bring down men.

In the Americas, early European explorers of the fifteenth century brought dogs with them. In areas they wished to seize, they sent trained dogs to attack indigenous peoples. Some were unarmed, while others had only spears or bows and arrows. Later explorers such as Christopher Columbus, Hernando de Soto, Juan Ponce de León, Hernán Cortés, and Vasco Núñez de Balboa relied on their war dogs for this same purpose. Even the US Army continued this brutal practice into the nineteenth century, using dogs to attack Seminole Indians during the Second Seminole War (1835–1842), a war fought by the US military and the Seminole Indians over territory in Florida. The army relied

Humans have long relied on dogs in hunting and on the battlefield. This wall panel from ancient Nineveh (a city in what later became northern Iraq) depicts huntsmen with their hounds. The relief dates to about 645–635 BCE.

on dogs to track and capture Seminole Indians and runaway slaves in the dense swamps of Florida and Louisiana. The Seminoles had traded weapons with the British during the War of 1812 (1812–1815), but the old muskets and rifles were no match for the more modern US Army artillery and war dogs.

By the twentieth century, the US military no longer used dogs to attack unarmed civilians. Instead, the military began to pair military working dogs (MWDs)—trained to scout for enemy soldiers and to guard military bases—with experienced handlers. The US military used few dogs during World War I, although the French and German armies deployed thousands. When the United States entered World War II in 1941, the government realized the value of war dogs and asked citizens to volunteer their dogs for military duty. Americans donated forty thousand dogs to Dogs for Defense. The military accepted about one-fourth of them as fit for duty. The military favored shepherds, huskies, malamutes, and Dobermans. With their short coats, Dobermans adapted especially well to the hot, muggy weather of the Pacific region.

When the Korean War began in 1950, the US military had only eighteen handlers and twenty-seven MWDs, all German shepherds. So the military trained about fifteen hundred dogs and their handlers to deploy to South Korea. The MWDs served as sentries, guarding US bases and camps to detect and prevent enemy soldiers from sneaking in at night. The dog and handler teams also worked with combat patrols, leading US soldiers along trails as they scouted out hidden enemy soldiers. In a military first, dogs and handlers went on night patrols.

North Korean soldiers had never seen such large animals and greatly feared them. If the North Koreans spotted a US patrol that included dogs, they tried to shoot the dogs before aiming at the US soldiers. The North Korean army frequently broadcast propaganda over loudspeakers set up on the North Korean side of the battlefield. Played at night, the broadcasts were meant to unnerve the American soldiers. One night the loudspeakers blared, "Yankee—take your dog and go home!"

Overall, the US Army estimated that MWDs reduced human casualties by 65 percent in the parts of the Korean peninsula where they served during the war. In 1953 the US Army recognized the dogs and their handlers for their service in Korea, saying: "The 26th Infantry Scout Dog Platoon is cited for exceptionally meritorious conduct in the performance of outstanding services in direct support of combat operations in Korea during the period 12 June 1951 to 15 January 1953."

JOHN BURNAM AND CLIPPER

"Directly to my front, Charlie [North Vietnamese soldiers] opened up with automatic rifle and machine gun fire," John Burnam remembered, writing about an ambush that he and his dog Clipper survived in 1967 during the Vietnam War (1957–1975). "Fortunately, I'd fallen near a small tree. I rolled behind it, Clipper at my side." Burnam and Clipper were caught between the crossfire of their own unit and the enemy. "Clipper and I lay only fifteen feet [4.5 m] from Charlie's entrenched positions. I could hear Vietnamese voices whispering from their foxholes. I knew Clipper heard them too, but he didn't make a sound."

Burnam joined the US Army in 1966 when he was eighteen years old. He went to Vietnam shortly after turning nineteen. After a knee injury that took him out of direct combat, the army sent Burnam to the capital city of Saigon to find a partner—a dog partner. Burnam walked along a string of kennels and stopped in front of an 80-pound (36 kg) German shepherd. They looked at each other, and something clicked between them. "If a dog could smile, Clipper smiled," Burnam said. "He was friendly, playful, intelligent, and energetic. Clipper was a four-footed soldier."

John Burnam's scout dog, Clipper, saved his life many times during the Vietnam War but was left behind at the end of the war. Burnam never knew exactly what became of him.

Burnam and Clipper trained with the 44th Infantry Platoon scout dog unit. They walked point, moving through terrain

THE NOT FORGOTTEN FOUNTAIN

John Burnam worked tirelessly to establish the Military Working Dog Teams National Monument at Lackland Air Force Base in San Antonio, Texas. The monument, built with donations raised by Burnam's Monument Foundation, was dedicated in 2013 and honors MWDs that worked in all branches of the US military.

Burnam also included a water fountain (*below*) for visiting dogs because he knew handlers would bring their dogs when they came to see the monument. The Not Forgotten Fountain, built to the side of the larger monument, features a soldier pouring water into his helmet, a common way of providing water to dogs in the field.

Ever since Vietnam, Burnam has held Clipper and the other dogs left behind there in his heart and mind. He wrote the inscription for the fountain. "In everlasting memory of all the heroic war dogs who served, died, and were left behind in the Vietnam War."

ahead of the soldiers hiking behind them. The leashed dog would go first, with the handler following, and then the rest of the unit. Together the dog and handler were a type of early warning system. It was one of the most dangerous jobs in Vietnam. "The enemy usually had the advantage of spotting the American point man first," Burnam said. "With a scout dog team, though, the tables were turned. We gained the advantage because a dog's instincts, vision, and sense of smell and hearing were hundreds of times more acute than a human's. Clipper was like a walking radar beam."

When Clipper smelled, heard, or saw something that worried him, he alerted, or stopped and stared in the direction of danger. His ears stood tall, and his body tilted forward. When Clipper alerted, Burnam knew something was wrong and warned his fellow soldiers that trouble lurked ahead. In *A Soldier's Best Friend*, the book Burnam wrote about his service in Vietnam, he describes how Clipper saved his life and the lives of numerous soldiers. Burnam and Clipper worked together for nearly a year until a previous knee injury started acting up, leading to Burnam's discharge.

Burnam knew the army assigned other handlers to work with Clipper after his discharge, but he never knew what happened to the dog or low long he may have lived. He does know that Clipper never came back home to the United States. At that time, the US military did not repatriate MWDs. The military feared that the dogs could not be retrained for civilian life and that it would be too expensive to bring them home. Many of the dogs were turned over to the South Vietnamese army, and others were euthanized.

Burnam described his final moments with Clipper. "The tragedy of it haunted me like a nightmare. I didn't know how to say goodbye to my best friend, so I looked into his big brown eyes and gave him one last loving farewell bear hug. I would keep Clipper alive in my heart for the rest of my life." Many years later, Burnam said, "This is the darkest chapter in the history of our nation's military working dog program. To have left the dogs behind in America's haste to leave was a tragedy of monumental consequences to the dogs."

Of the four thousand MWDs that served in Vietnam, only about two hundred returned home. The Vietnam Veterans Memorial Wall in Washington, DC, holds the names of more than fifty-eight thousand Americans killed in Vietnam. "Without [the dogs], there would have been another ten thousand names on the Wall," Ron Aiello, president and founder of the US War Dog Association said.

AFGHANISTAN AND IRAQ

On September 11, 2001, al-Qaeda terrorists hijacked four US civilian airplanes. They flew two of the planes into New York City's World Trade Center and one into the Pentagon in Arlington, Virginia. Passengers stormed hijackers on the fourth plane—apparently headed for Washington, DC—forcing it to crash into a Pennsylvania field. Those attacks, which killed nearly three thousand people, triggered the country's longest wars. Just weeks after the 9/11 attacks, the United States bombed and later invaded sites in Afghanistan believed to be training areas for the terrorists. Two years later, the US military invaded Iraq, hoping to topple the government of dictator Saddam Hussein. US leaders claimed that Iraq possessed nuclear weapons of mass destruction.

The war in Iraq ended in 2011, but the war in Afghanistan continues as of 2018. In both countries, the US military relied heavily on MWDs and their handlers. Each military dog team saves between 150 and 200 soldiers during the dog's working life. The dogs sniff out concealed bombs and other weapons, and they alert their handlers to hidden enemy soldiers. Four eyes. Two hearts. One team. The dog and handler live together, eat together, play together, often sleep together, and risk their lives for each other every day while in a war zone.

An estimated thirty-two hundred MWDs served in the US military at the height of the Iraq and Afghanistan wars. This

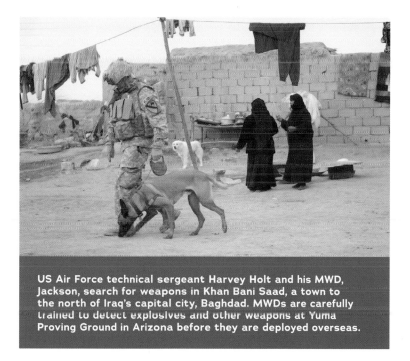

US Air Force technical sergeant Harvey Holt and his MWD, Jackson, search for weapons in Khan Bani Saad, a town to the north of Iraq's capital city, Baghdad. MWDs are carefully trained to detect explosives and other weapons at Yuma Proving Ground in Arizona before they are deployed overseas.

includes those dogs that served at US military bases around the world during that time. Dogs require training to work in the hot desert and mountain terrains of Iraq and Afghanistan. They had to learn the odors of a dozen or more types of explosives, both old and new, including trinitrotoluene (TNT—the material used in dynamite), C4 plastic explosive, ammonium nitrate, potassium chlorate, and smokeless powder. They learned to tolerate the deafening chaos of helicopters, tanks, and combat, as well as parachuting out of a plane while strapped to their handlers' chests.

GLORY HOUNDS

A day's mission in Iraq or Afghanistan usually involved searching for improvised explosive devices (IEDs) hidden along roads under mounds of rubble and trash. IEDs are crude homemade explosives that a person can trigger with trip wires or electronic signals such as a simple cell phone call. Other IEDs are buried in the sand or set to explode when someone steps on a hidden pressure plate. Enemy combatants place IEDs in vehicles and deserted houses, and they wear IEDs inside suicide vests. The US military estimates that IEDs have caused about two-thirds of American deaths and injuries in Iraq and Afghanistan.

Most MWDs deployed to Afghanistan and Iraq were dual-purpose dogs. While they patrolled and attacked enemy soldiers, the largest part of their work was sniffing out bombs. The 2013 Animal Planet documentary *Glory Hounds* follows four dog teams as they

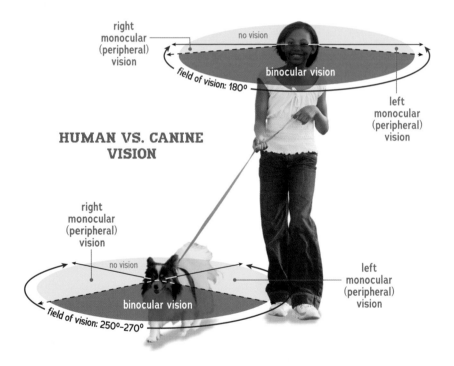

right monocular (peripheral) vision

no vision

binocular vision

field of vision: 180°

left monocular (peripheral) vision

HUMAN VS. CANINE VISION

right monocular (peripheral) vision

no vision

binocular vision

field of vision: 250°–270°

left monocular (peripheral) vision

Dogs have a much wider field of vision than humans do. MWDs rely on sight for some of their duties. And with their keen sense of smell, they sniff out bombs, IEDs, and other explosives.

locate insurgents (rebels fighting against an established government) and explosives. MWDs are much more than furry bomb detectors, however. They also search cars and trucks, deserted mud huts, roadsides, and rocky grain and grape fields in which enemy insurgents hide. Dogs protect their handlers, guard American bases, and protect American lives. Dog teams routinely go outside the wire—leaving the safety of the base to conduct missions with their handlers. "Our goal is to . . . save someone's life, especially American lives," marine Kent Ferrell said of his work with MWD Zora. "That's our job."

Just how good are MWDs at saving lives? Technical Sergeant Justin Kitts received a Bronze Star in 2011 for his work in Afghanistan with his dog Dyngo. The military credits Kitts and Dyngo with having protected thirty thousand US and coalition forces (countries such as Germany, Italy, and the United Kingdom that are allies of the United States). The team also protected civilians during their one thousand hours outside the wire. During those operations, Dyngo discovered nearly 400 pounds (181 kg) of explosives and several IEDs.

Brandon Liebert, who deployed overseas with his dog Monty, described a particularly good day in Iraq when they searched an abandoned house. In one room, they found an antiaircraft gun and more than six hundred antiaircraft rounds. "I was so proud of [Monty], and he was really happy, because he knew he did a great job," said Liebert. Before MWDs deployed to Iraq and Afghanistan, only about half of all IEDs were discovered before they exploded. After dogs joined the soldiers, the detection rate increased to 80 percent.

CHARLES OGIN AND RROBIEK

Army staff sergeant Charles Ogin and his MWD Rrobiek have served together since 2014 at an American base in Baghdad, Iraq. (The double r's in Rrobiek's name indicate that he was born at the MWD breeding program at Lackland Air Force Base in San Antonio, Texas.) Rrobiek is a patrol and explosive detection dog. His job is to ensure intruders and their bombs don't make it onto the base. "We're responsible for checking all vehicular traffic for explosive odor while on shift," Ogin said.

"We also help to protect VIPs [very important persons, such as visiting dignitaries]. In 2015 we had a temporary duty assignment to Kenya [in Africa], where we worked with local security forces and the American Secret Service to ensure the safety of President Barack Obama when he visited the country." Ogin and Rrobiek searched hotels, stadiums, parking garages, and routes the president might travel for bombs.

In 2017 a military journalist interviewed Ogin about his relationship with Rrobiek. "He's a piece of equipment in the Army's eyes, but he has his own personality, his own quirks. He's very set in his ways, kind of like a person," Ogin said. "I have a dog that's loyal. He's willing to work until he dies and he's willing to defend me. I can't say that about every soldier. . . . But that dog will defend me until I die." How do Ogin and Rrobiek spend their off-duty time? "We spend it training in obedience, practicing finding explosives, and playing with toys!" Ogin hopes to adopt Rrobiek when the dog retires.

PAWS ON THE GROUND

Like Rrobiek, nearly 15 percent of America's MWDs begin their lives at Lackland Air Force Base. The military purchases the rest from European dog breeders. Lackland breeds only Belgian Malinois dogs. Stewart Hilliard heads Lackland's breeding program and believes they're the best dogs for the job. "The breed suffers from fewer genetically-based medical problems than does the other possible breed for us—German Shepherds—with lower rates of hip dysplasia [an abnormal formation of the hip socket] and spinal problems," Hilliard said. The puppies are socialized from birth. They spend several months in civilian foster homes to experience a wide variety of situations.

MEGAN LEAVEY AND REX

The 2017 movie *Megan Leavey* tells the story of US Marine corporal Megan Leavey and her MWD Rex. Critics said, "*Megan Leavey* honors its real-life subjects with a sensitive, uplifting, drama." Leavey was one of ten handlers with whom MWD Rex worked throughout his career. She and Rex completed one hundred missions during their two tours in Iraq. Their luck ran out in 2006 when an IED exploded outside Ramadi. The explosion knocked Leavey unconscious and damaged blood vessels inside her eyes and ears. All she could think about was Rex. "I remember waking up and pulling my leash and thinking, 'Oh, my God, please be something on the other end of this leash!" Both Leavey and Rex survived their injuries, although it took a year of recovery and rehabilitation.

Leavey was discharged in 2007 with a Purple Heart. However, the US Marines assigned Rex to a new handler. Leavey tried for five years to adopt Rex. The Marine Corps considered Rex such a valuable asset that they repeatedly denied her request and assigned the dog to new handlers. When Rex became ill, the Marine Corps finally released him to Leavey on April 6, 2012.

During his retirement ceremony at Camp Pendleton, California, Rex received a citation that said in part, "MWD Rex performed his duties in an exemplary and highly professional manner. MWD Rex's enthusiasm, initiative, and loyal devotion to duty reflected great credit upon himself, and were in keeping with the finest traditions of the Marine Corps and the United States Naval Service."

Rex died of cancer just a few months later. "I am so grateful for the last eight months I got to spend with my partner and my best friend," Leavey said. "Rex got to swim in a pool and play with my other dogs . . . and sleep in a cozy bed next to me every night. . . . He knew I was with him the whole time and I laid next to him & held him & spoke to him & he was at peace in the end. He is now my guardian angel."

Dogs such as these Belgian Malinois in Lackland's puppy program are frequently evaluated to see if they will be suited for the base's MWD program when they are older.

Training begins at Lackland when pups are about seven months old. The pups learn to hunt for toys and to obey simple commands such as sit and stay. Obedience is vital. A dog that does not immediately obey its handler puts both animal and human in jeopardy. Trainers also expose the puppies to situations they will encounter in a combat zone, such as gunfire and loud aircraft. The dogs become used to being in large, bumpy vehicles and in strange buildings and skilled at dashing through tunnels, up and down steps, and across elevated platforms.

When the dogs are one year old, experts assess them to be sure they have what it takes to become official MWDs. Hilliard said potential MWDs must display three basic traits. "First, they must have a strong predatory drive. This behavior is especially important for search dogs and bomb-detecting dogs. We harness their instinct to chase stuff that moves, to pick it up, and to hold it in their mouths." The other two drives are the bite drive and environmental stability.

"The bite drive is the need to grab stuff and hold on. Dogs with a strong bite drive love to play tug of war," Hilliard explains. "This drive is vital for patrol dogs that chase, apprehend [catch], and hold on to fleeing suspects. Lastly, dogs with strong environmental stability are confident and bold. New environments, scary noises, or strange people will not intimidate them," he said.

All MWDs learn how to patrol—to search for and catch an enemy if the handler gives the order. They also learn to detect either illegal drugs or the IEDs widely used in Afghanistan, Iraq, and the combat zones of Syria, where civil war broke out in 2011. Handlers never train a dog to detect both IEDs and drugs because of the potential for confusion and injury.

Dogs in training receive only praise and a toy—usually a Kong toy—when they perform well. Whether training a dog to detect drugs or IEDs, trainers expose the dogs to a variety of odors. These include marijuana or cocaine for drug dogs, and bomb-making chemicals for IED dogs. Then the trainers hide drugs or chemicals in vehicles and rooms, heaping praise and love on the dog and a few minutes of playtime with each successful find. In a "final exam," the MWD must locate a tiny amount of drugs or IED-making chemicals hidden in a large cargo plane or in a vehicle within a minute or two while ignoring distracting odors.

MWDs still have a lot to learn before they are ready to go paws on the ground in a war zone. Hundreds of MWDs and their handlers have worked at the Yuma Proving Ground in the hot Arizona desert. There they train in mocked-up villages, mosques (Islamic houses of worship), and roads that are similar to the Middle Eastern environments they will face when deployed. Dogs learn to ride in tanks, trucks, and planes and to tolerate being hoisted from the ground with their handlers to a hovering helicopter. Fitted with doggles (goggles for dogs) and a muzzle (to prevent the dog from snapping at the air and possibly injuring itself), the dog is strapped to

US Air Force staff sergeant Angela Lowe leads Szultan through an obstacle course in 2014 at the joint US Air Force/Navy base in Charleston, South Carolina. The obstacle course helps prepare MWDs for the challenges they will face while on duty.

his handler's chest and hauled up. "He has full and total trust in me as the handler and knows that I am not going to let any harm get to him," Master Sergeant Bruce Brickleff said of his MWD Buri after multiple practice hoists.

ONE DOG HANDLER'S STORY

Angela Lowe joined the military in 2006 when she was seventeen, so young that her mom had to give written permission. "My best friend in high school and I were watching the military channel one day after school. We looked at each other and decided it would be cool to join the Air Force," she said. "I saw a picture of a dog handler on a recruitment brochure and decided that was the job I wanted, even though I had never owned a dog."

Lowe worked in air force security for six years before she became a dog handler. Only about 10 percent of handlers are women. "It's a very male-dominated career field," said Lowe, who's stationed at the joint US Air Force/Navy base in Charleston, South Carolina. She works with her fourth dog, Szultan, a large German shepherd with a mind of his own. "I was out in a field with another trainer one day. I wanted to try some off-leash training. As soon as Szultan felt the leash come off, he said, 'See ya lady. I'm outa here.' He took off running through the woods and didn't listen to a word I said. I couldn't even get his attention with a toy. It took twenty minutes to catch him. We were still building rapport and trust at the time."

After a few weeks, the bond between Lowe and Szultan grew stronger. "He's a funny dog with a weird personality. We know each other's moods. Some days, he just wakes up on the wrong side of the kennel, so to speak. He'll growl at me one minute, then come up to me and want some love. Now I have a bond with him like no other MWD that I've worked. He's a quick learner and will do anything I show him. It's an amazing feeling seeing your dog learn new things. I'm his first handler, and that's a pretty cool bond. One of my goals as a handler is to make sure when I pass the leash off to someone else, they have a really great working dog."

CHAPTER 7

LUCKY CHARMS AND ATOMIC PIGS

I have frequently seen [Union] Generals Grant, Sherman [and others] . . . raise their hats as they passed Old Abe, which always brought a cheer from the regiment and then the Eagle would spread his wings . . . and he did look magnificent at such times.

—David McLain, keeper of Old Abe, a Civil War mascot,
late nineteenth century

The English word *mascot* comes from the French word *mascotte*, referring to an object that brings good luck. Soldiers and sailors have adopted mascots for several hundred years. During wartime, animal mascots improve morale, provide comfort and friendship, and distract soldiers and sailors from the fears and anxiety they feel as they face danger. Military men and women become extremely attached to their mascots, which have included foxes, pigs, a monkey, a donkey, dogs and cats, pigeons, an antelope, a goose, and a chicken called Charlotte.

THE CAT THAT SAVED A SHIP

The little black-and-white tuxedo cat called Simon enjoyed strolling across the laps of dinner guests. He liked to sit on the nautical chart as the ship's captain plotted a course. He liked to sleep with the captain in his quarters. And Simon liked to catch the occasional mouse. Mostly, he enjoyed visiting with the crew and playing with

his friend, Peggy, a small terrier. After all, that was his job, because Simon and Peggy were mascots.

World War II had ended in 1945, and the British warship *Amethyst* remained stationed in China to help guard the British Embassy in Nanking. After World War II, Chinese Nationalists and Communists fought a civil war (1945–1949) for control of the nation. On April 20, 1949, as the *Amethyst* headed up the Yangtze River to deliver supplies to the embassy, the Communists opened fire. Bullets and shells hit the vessel fifty-four times, killing the captain. The sailors found Simon unconscious, with singed fur, burned whiskers, a punctured lung, and numerous shrapnel injuries.

The *Amethyst* had run aground on a sandbar during the brief attack. The crew managed to move it off the sandbar to repair the damage (and Simon). For one hundred days, Communist forces kept an eye on the *Amethyst* to make sure it did not continue on its way to the British Embassy. The shelling had driven rats from their usual hiding places, and within days, they were devouring stores of food. The crew was at risk of starvation. The Communists would not allow the delivery of provisions to the *Amethyst*. Instead, they were willing to wait for the ship to surrender when the sailors got hungry enough. The British crew moved Simon—by this time fully recovered—to the storage rooms below deck where the rats lived. Simon captured and killed at least one of the supersized rats—grown fat and lazy from eating the crew's provisions—each day.

One dark night, the crew of the *Amethyst* saw a chance to escape. The ship sneaked behind another passing vessel on its way out to sea and hid in its wake. The *Amethyst* made it safely into international waters, limping to Hong Kong for major repairs before returning with Simon to England. Simon didn't survive long, however. While in quarantine in England, he died of a heart condition that had gone unnoticed. Simon was the only cat ever awarded a Dickin Medal, in 1949, shortly after his death. His Dickin citation said, "Simon, neuter cat, served on HMS *Amethyst* during the Yangtze Incident, disposing of many rats though wounded by shell blast. Throughout the Incident, his behavior was of the highest order." Simon was buried in a cat-sized coffin covered by a British flag amid bouquets of flowers from admiring fans.

GOATS AND EAGLES AND BEARS, OH MY!

In the Revolutionary War, a goat helped lead the British to victory against the Americans at the 1775 Battle of Bunker Hill in Boston, Massachusetts. Or so the story goes. Actually, the goat just wandered onto the battlefield and ended up parading with the British regiment after the battle. Because the British won the battle, they considered the goat to be such good luck that they adopted him as their mascot. The practice of drafting goats as British military mascots was born.

During a visit to Caernarfon Castle in North Wales in 2010, Queen Elizabeth II met Dai Davies from the 1st Royal Welch (Welsh) Fusiliers (an infantry regiment) and the regimental goat William Windsor.

Queen Victoria (1819–1901) and Queen Elizabeth II (1926–) are among the British monarchs who presented longhaired Kashmir goats as military mascots to the Royal Welch (Welsh) Fusiliers, a British infantry regiment. The goats, all called William Windsor (or Billy, for short) after the British royal family name, are promoted to lance corporal if they do well at their assigned duty of leading parades.

Later in US history, during the Civil War era, an eagle took center stage. In 1861 an Ojibwa man traded his young pet eagle to some Wisconsin settlers for a bushel of corn. Soon after, the settlers offered the eagle to the 8th Wisconsin Volunteer Infantry Regiment. The men called the bird Old Abe, after President Abraham Lincoln. The soldiers carried Old Abe into battle on a perch, where he watched from the sidelines, screeching and flapping his wings. The eagle accompanied his regiment—renamed the Eagle Regiment—into thirty-six battles during the Civil War. After the war, Old Abe lived in a two-bedroom apartment, complete with a custom bathtub, in the capitol building in Madison, Wisconsin, for twenty years until his death in 1881.

More than sixty years later, a bear came onto a different battle scene. In World War II, the British formed the Polish 22nd Artillery Supply Company from a large group of Polish prisoners of war whom Soviet leader Joseph Stalin had released for that purpose. In 1942 the men passed through much of the Middle East, heading to Egypt to meet with British forces. While going through Iran, the soldiers came upon a shepherd boy with an orphan bear cub. The men bought the cub for their mascot and called him Voytek. The cub immediately adapted to life in the army. "He was like a child, like a small dog," Wojciech Narebski, a former company soldier said. "He was given milk from a bottle, like a baby. So therefore he felt that these soldiers are nearly his parents, and therefore he trusted in us and was very friendly."

Like most bears, Voytek would consume nearly everything he could get his paws on. He grew to be 440 pounds (200 kg), so big that he could no longer ride in jeeps. Instead, he rode in the rear of big supply trucks. Voytek enjoyed boxing and wrestling with his human comrades. But his primary job was to lift morale. Voytek became a hero after he confronted a thief in camp one night. The soldiers arrested the thief.

In 1943 the 22nd Artillery soldiers joined with a larger group of Polish and British soldiers and sailed from Egypt to Italy to fight alongside the British 8th Army to push out the Germans. To make sure Voytek could go with them, some of the men forged military papers for the bear and officially drafted him into the Polish army. During a major battle at Monte Cassino, Italy, Voytek worked for hours, carrying crates of ammunition to the cannons on the front lines. The sound of gunfire didn't seem to bother the bear at all.

Voytek was so beloved that the Polish 22nd Artillery Supply Company adopted an image of a bear carrying a missile as its official badge. After the war, Voytek spent the rest of his life at the Edinburgh Zoo in Scotland, where he was a popular attraction. Former members of the company loved to visit Voytek and talk to him in Polish. Voytek never lost his gentle ways, and he died in 1963 when he was twenty-one years old.

The US Army has many unofficial animal mascots but only three official ones. Two mules represent the US Military Academy in West Point, New York. A borzoi—a Russian wolfhound—represents the 27th Infantry Regiment based at Schofield Barracks in Hawaii. Why a Russian dog in Hawaii? When the unit served in Siberia in 1918 at the end of World War I, the Russian Bolsheviks (members of a revolutionary workers' political party) had so admired the Americans that they nicknamed the regiment's men "wolfhounds."

The US Marines have used English bulldogs—all named Chesty— as their official mascot since 1922. Each Chesty gets a number. In 2013 Sergeant Chesty XIII retired from service, and Private First Class Chesty XIV succeeded him. The Marine Corps promoted

GLOWWORMS IN THE TRENCHES

Soldiers huddling in the muddy, murky trenches of World War I turned to luminous fireflies called glowworms in their darkest hours. Men collected fireflies or their larvae (which also glow) by the thousands and stored them in jars. It took only a few glowworms to provide enough light at night for officers to study battle plans and intelligence reports, for soldiers to reread treasured letters from home, and for pigeoneers to write messages for their birds to carry the next day. About two dozen glowworms emit about the same amount of light as a lantern and were far less likely to be spotted by the enemy in a distant trench.

Outgoing US Marine Corps mascot Sergeant Chesty XIII (*right*) greets the incoming Marine mascot, Private First Class Chesty XIV, during a 2013 ceremony in Washington, DC. The English bulldog has been the breed of choice for the Marine's mascot since the 1950s. Each is named Chesty in honor of the most decorated marine in US history, General Lewis "Chesty" Puller (1898–1971).

Chesty XIV to corporal during an official ceremony in 2014 for being "a good boy."

Sometimes soldiers took an enemy's mascot as a prisoner of war, but the soldiers usually treated the animals well. For example, in 1943 British sailors rescued a small wire-haired terrier from a German U-boat they had sunk. The new owner named the dog Adelbert and claimed it soon began acting more English than German. The British navy also rescued a fox terrier named Fritz, according to the name on its tag, from another sunken German ship. His new owners—finding the name Fritz to be too German—quickly changed his name to Fred. Then came Fritz, a German Great Pyrenees mountain dog. A British officer captured Fritz during the D-day landings in Normandy, France, on June 6, 1944. The British sent Fritz back to England where he nearly was put down under Britain's tough quarantine regulations. A British Wren (a member of the Women's Royal Naval Service) paid the hefty quarantine fee to save Fritz. It took Fritz a while to become used to hearing English rather than German. Fritz became the mascot to the Royal Hampshire Regiment and wore an embroidered coat during regimental ceremonies.

DISPOSABLE DOGS

Many animal mascots enjoyed pampered lives. Yet militaries have used animals in experiments, often with fatal outcomes for the animals. For example, beginning in 1930, soldiers in the Soviet army trained large dogs—usually German shepherds—to carry bombs to enemy tanks. These experimental anti-tank dog units officially became part of the Soviet army in 1935. Initially, the plan was for the dogs to leave their bombs at the targets—intended to be German tanks—and to retreat until a timer set off the explosives. But often the dogs got confused and ran back to their own side. They dropped the bombs, whose explosions killed Soviet soldiers instead of enemy soldiers. So the Soviet military developed a new plan in which the dogs would not be required to drop the bombs. Instead, the bombs would go off when the dog reached the tank, and the dogs as well as the enemy would die in the explosions.

How do you train a dog to deliver a bomb? The Soviets kept the dogs in cages in a state of perpetual hunger. Trainers placed food under Soviet tanks and then released the caged dogs to get the food. The dogs learned to associate food with the underside of tanks. In the next stage of training, trainers turned the tank motors on and left them idling while the dogs got their food. Lastly, soldiers fired weapons around the dogs as they ran toward the food. In this way, the dogs became used to battlefield conditions.

Once training was completed, the Soviets fitted large dogs with backpacks, complete with 22 to 26 pounds (10 to 12 kg) of explosives—enough to blow up or badly damage a tank. A wooden lever extended from each backpack so that when a dog dived under the enemy tank to seek food, the lever struck the bottom of the tank and detonated the charge (and the dog).

The plan didn't work as well as the Soviets had hoped. During World War II, the Germans used a different fuel in their tanks than did the Soviets, and the unfamiliar odor sometimes confused the dogs. Many ran back to their handlers instead of going under the German tanks. The wooden lever would brush against a friendly person or object, setting off the explosives. The dog experiments apparently greatly demoralized the Soviet soldiers, and after 1942, the Soviets seldom used the animals to set off explosives.

ATOMIC ANIMALS

The Soviet army wasn't the only military force to experiment with animals. The US Navy experimented with bats during World War II. Researchers attached small bombs to the loose skin on the bats' chests and set the bombs to go off at a specific time. Bats can carry more than their own weight in flight, and carrying a tiny bomb was no problem for them. The plan was for American pilots to drop the bomb-toting bats over Japanese villages to set them on fire. In one test near Carlsbad, New Mexico, armed bats accidentally were released. They set the Carlsbad Army Airfield Auxiliary Air Base on fire on May 15, 1943, and incinerated the test range. The US government canceled the $2 million project and devoted funds to developing the atomic bomb instead.

In 1945 the United States beat the Germans and the Russians in the race to build an atomic bomb. US B-29 bombers dropped two of them on the cities of Hiroshima and Nagasaki, Japan, in August 1945. The devastation was beyond anything the world had ever witnessed, and Japan surrendered within days of the second bomb, ending World War II.

The bombs killed huge numbers of people immediately, but the long-term effects of radiation were unknown. US military officials and scientists wanted to develop better atomic bombs and to learn more about them. So the military set up testing facilities in the Marshall

Islands in the Pacific Ocean about halfway between Hawaii and Australia. On July 1, 1946, the US Navy would detonate the first of sixty-seven atomic (and eventually hydrogen) bombs in the Marshall Islands, most of them in the Bikini Atoll.

For the first bomb, the navy anchored the USS *Burleson*, nicknamed *Noah's Ark*, in Bikini Atoll. Aboard were 146 pigs, 176 goats, fifty-seven guinea pigs, and 3,139 rats and mice. The plan was to learn how the radiation released from the bomb's explosion would affect living creatures. Animal lovers around the world protested the use of animals in this

Seaman Second Class Dale Lipps (*left*) and Seaman Second Class Richard M. Williamson (*right*) arrive in the United States with Pig #311 and Goat BO Plenty three months after the July 1946 Able explosion. Both animals were exposed to radioactive fallout as part of the weapons testing experiment.

experiment, and public uproar forced the military to reject its original plan to include dogs. William H. P. Blandy, the American admiral in charge of the program, said, "We regret that some of these animals may be sacrificed. . . . The Army and Navy simply can't be starry-eyed about this phase of the experiment."

Before detonating the first bomb (code name Able), each animal had been tattooed with an identification number because the explosion was likely to blow off tags or other identification markers. Some goats were shaved to see if the radiation would affect military personnel with buzz cuts. Other goats were covered with sunblock, and several pigs were dressed in navy uniforms to see if lotions or cloth offered protection against radiation. Sailors placed the animals aboard several damaged and useless ships that the navy had towed to the area and anchored in the Bikini lagoon. They waited to see what would happen when the atomic bomb exploded.

A military press release said of the event, "It is not the intention to kill a large portion of the animals since dead animals are of less value for study. We want radiation-sick animals, but not radiation-dead animals." That was not the outcome, however. About 10 percent of the animals died instantly during the explosion. Almost all the others died within a few months of the explosion from radiation-related illnesses. On July 15, just two weeks after the first test, newspaper headlines screamed, "A report that Bikini test animals have begun 'dying like flies' came today from the USS *Burleson*, highly-secret animal ship from which reporters have been barred." While the atomic explosion was not a secret, the military didn't want reporters to see the sick and dying animals that had been regrouped on the *Burleson*.

One test animal that survived the explosion was Animal #311, a young pig. She deliberately had been locked in an officers' bathroom on the Japanese cruiser *Sakawa*, a leaky and rat-infested ship that the Japanese government had turned over to the US Navy as a prize of war. The cruiser was near the center of the explosion. The blast set the *Sakawa* on fire, and the vessel sank the next day. Several hours later, sailors found Pig #311 swimming in the Bikini lagoon, seemingly unhurt. The metal walls of the bathroom likely saved her life. The navy sent the pig to the Naval Medical Research Institute in Maryland for examination. Other than a bad temper and a low blood count, the pig recovered fully. She ended her days at a zoo in Washington, DC, where she grew from a 50-pound (23 kg) piglet to a 600-pound (272 kg) porker. Despite attempts at breeding, Pig #311 never had babies. Doctors believed her infertility was a result of radiation exposure.

FOR THE GOOD OF MANKIND?

Since the Vietnam War, the US military has tested surgical techniques on live animals, a practice called live tissue trauma training. After anesthetizing the animals, researchers shot the animals, stabbed them, burned them with napalm fuel, amputated their limbs, or sliced open their bodies. The tests allowed medics to train on living animals. In theory, this made them better able to perform lifesaving procedures on soldiers injured by gunfire, bombs, and the IEDs used so often in twenty-first-century battles. In 2012 the US Department of Defense (DoD) used nine to ten thousand pigs and goats along with a few monkeys in these experiments.

According to an NBC interview with two unidentified marines in 2017, the live trauma tissue training is still going on. Marines who participate in the training board a bus at California's Camp Pendleton and are driven to an undisclosed off-site location two hours away. The interviewed marines said that medical corpsmen and Special Forces soldiers are told to wear civilian clothes for the training, and "before they get on the bus, they take everyone's cell phone away" so no one can take photos of the procedures.

Animal rights organizations, including People for the Ethical Treatment of Animals (PETA), have lobbied the DoD for years to end the practice. In 2015 the US military stopped most of its live animal experiments. They shifted to realistic human dummies that civilian doctors and nurses use in their training. Yet the US military still is allowed to mimic battle conditions by shooting and blowing up anesthetized goats and pigs to see how severe trauma affects living creatures. PETA and others continue to push for a complete ban on military animal testing. The movement gained greater support in 2017 when tens of thousands of physicians, military veterans, and members of the US Congress spoke out against it.

CHAPTER 8

ANIMALS IN THE TWENTY-FIRST CENTURY

Most animals who have died have no memorial. Sick, wounded, starved, slaughtered, they have perished as though they had never been. The only way we can repay them is to treat them with more kindness in peace, and hope that in the future they are drawn as little as possible into our wars.

—*Jilly Cooper*, Animals in War, *1983*

The nature of war has changed greatly over the centuries. People no longer take elephants into battle or set pigs on fire to scare away enemies. Soldiers no longer march horses, camels, and mules laden with heavy equipment into combat and to potential death. Pigeon fanciers hold races for their birds instead of sending them off to brave bullets and bombs as they carry messages. Armored tanks, gun-toting helicopters, bomb-carrying jets and drones, and electronic communication mean that far fewer animals participate in human conflicts. Yet some do continue to serve.

WAR DOGS COME HOME

About twenty-eight hundred MWDs remain in service, according to Ron Aiello. Of those, the US military says about sixteen hundred MWDs are serving in Afghanistan. The others are in other countries and at American bases around the world. Will the military continue to need MWDs in the future?

An American MWD in Parwan Province, Afghanistan, wears doggles to protect his eyes as a helicopter takes off, kicking up dust and debris.

Emily Pieracci, a veterinarian who has provided care to MWDs, said, "MWDs work on pretty much every military base worldwide. They serve as drug and explosive detectors, as well as general security for the bases. MWDs will continue to be a valuable asset for the military." According to John Burnam, "MWDs have proven their worth since they were deployed on the battlefields of WWII. Today, MWDs are saving lives and protecting American assets in the Middle East and here in the United States where they patrol US bases for drugs and intruders. This makes them irreplaceable for the foreseeable future."

As MWDs become too old or too disabled to continue their work, what happens to them? Unlike the millions of animals that served in wartime before them, many war dogs live out the balance of their lives back at home, happy and comfortable. Former president Bill Clinton signed Robby's Law—named after a MWD that died before his handler could adopt him—in 2000. The law required that military dogs be returned to civilian life whenever possible. The Department of Defense says it has a cradle-to-grave philosophy for its dogs. "These dogs are treated like Marines," Bill Childress, manager for the Marine Corps MWD program, said. "We bring everybody home." Former handlers nearly always adopt MWDs after military veterinarians fully evaluate the dogs' physical and mental health to be certain they can adapt to civilian life.

MWDs have a tougher job in twenty-first-century warfare than they had in earlier decades. In the Middle East, in particular, they work in extremely hot deserts and very cold mountains. They jump over fences and trenches, cross wobbly bridges, climb stairs, and run over rocky terrain. The physical wear and tear on a dog's body is significant. So the average age of retiring MWDs has dropped from ten years to eight and a half years.

Meet Iva, Maci, and Dyngo. These dogs completed their Middle East service, and they are spending their well-earned retirement in the United States.

DUSTIN WEEKS AND IVA. "Iva is a very vocal dog and affectionate. She loves to be petted and will bring a toy and put it in your lap to get attention," said Sergeant Dustin Weeks, stationed at Columbus Air Force Base in Mississippi. Weeks and

Dustin Weeks adopted his MWD, Iva (*right*), in 2015 after serving with her in Afghanistan.

Iva—an all-black German shepherd—served in Afghanistan together. "Our most important task was to find and clear IEDs from roads and bridges, and to find hidden weapon caches." Weeks and Iva also served a tour in the Middle Eastern nation of Qatar. Weeks said that when not deployed in a war zone, "the team searches commercial vehicles for drugs, and conducts patrols throughout the base. The biggest advantage of having a MWD is the psychological deterrent."

Weeks adopted Iva in 2015, and she fits well into his family. "I have two dachshunds at home and she gets along just fine with them. I also have a young daughter who loves to play with her. Iva has full access to my house and a doggy door that leads into a fenced-in back yard." Weeks is proud of the work Iva has done. Along with her deployments, Iva has accompanied the US Secret Service to guard American dignitaries when they traveled outside the United States. "She has been a true asset to the United States Air Force."

KARL STEFANOWICZ AND MACI. "Maci is a 73-pound [33 kg] black German shepherd who thinks he's a lap dog," said Staff Sergeant Karl Stefanowicz. "All he wants to do is run around and play. I call him a wrecking ball because he has no sense of how big he actually is." Like Iva, Maci worked in Afghanistan as an explosive-detection dog with another handler before he became Stefanowicz's partner. "Maci is a true war hero and has saved many lives," he says. He and Maci served at the American base in Oman for six months until Maci developed pain in his hips. A veterinarian decided that Maci could no longer serve in the military.

Stefanowicz adopted Maci in 2014, and he fits well into his new life. "Maci is just another family member. He has his own bed and relaxes with the rest of us. Maci lies down next to our baby and watches over him. You can see he's bonded with the baby already. Maci learned quickly he needed to protect my family like he did me." Stefanowicz adds, "While we are deployed and away from home and family, these dogs are our family. They keep us sane. They are the real heroes and our best friends."

LUCCA WINS A MEDAL

MWD Lucca made history in April 2016 when she became the first American dog to receive the Dickin Medal, the highest military honor for animals in the world. While deployed to Afghanistan in 2012 with her handler Juan Rodriguez—a member of the US Army Special Forces—Lucca lost a front leg when she stepped on a bomb. Army veterinarians in Afghanistan treated her, and within ten days of her injury, Lucca had learned to walk on three legs. At the award ceremony near Buckingham Palace in London, England, Jan McLoughlin, director of the organization awarding the medal, said, "Lucca's conspicuous gallantry and devotion to duty makes her a hugely deserving recipient of . . . the Dickin Medal. Her ability and determination to seek out arms and explosives preserved human life amid some of the world's fiercest military conflicts."

In London, on April 5, 2016, Gunnery Sergeant Christopher Willingham of Tuscaloosa, Alabama, shakes hands with retired MWD Lucca, after the dog received the Dickin Medal for animal bravery. The twelve-year-old German shepherd lost her leg in 2012 in Afghanistan when she was searching for IEDs. When a device detonated, she instantly lost her front left leg.

REBECCA FRANKEL, AND DYNGO. Occasionally a person outside the military gets to adopt an MWD. Rebecca Frankel has written extensively about MWDs since 2010 in her role as journalist and editor for *Foreign Policy* magazine. In 2016 she adopted Dyngo, a Belgian Malinois that had served multiple tours in Afghanistan. She first met Dyngo in 2012 at Lackland Air Force Base in Texas. "While I was reporting, I tried my best to not to have favorite dogs," she said. "But I found that's nearly impossible. . . . It's no exaggeration to say that I dug Dyngo right from the get-go."

After adoption, it took a while for Dyngo to get used to civilian life. "He didn't understand what we were supposed to be doing," Frankel said. "For so long he had one routine and a single purpose that he trained for every day. He had a job for which he was rewarded, a job where all the rules were clear. It wasn't easy for him to adjust to something entirely different." Even a simple walk had its problems at first. "It's not as if I could tell him, no, we're not hunting for bombs today; this is just a trip to the bathroom!" Sometimes Frankel thinks about the amazing things Dyngo has done in his life and the places he's been. "I wonder what he thinks of his life now," she muses.

Frankel wants people to know how truly remarkable war dogs are. "Their contribution to the military is vital to saving lives—whether it's saving a patrol from stepping on an IED in Afghanistan, or patrolling an airport in Colorado. Their ability surpasses modern technology. But it's even more important that we understand how we humans harness it. It's not through dominance or discipline, but with respect and compassion—positive reinforcement, patience, commitment, attentiveness, and ultimately, love."

RATS AT WORK

Unlike IEDs, which are often very simple in design, land mines are military-quality bombs. Traditional armies and unconventional warriors such as guerrillas, rebels, and insurgents have buried land mines for decades and still do in armed conflicts in Iraq, Yemen, Afghanistan, and Syria. Yet when the battles are over, land mines usually remain. Land mines not only kill many innocent civilians, but they also prevent farming of great swathes of valuable land. Increasingly, land mines have become a serious issue in Africa, including Nigeria, Tunisia, Zimbabwe, and especially Libya, where experts say thousands of explosives have been buried. And millions of land mines are still in place from the Vietnam War in Cambodia, Vietnam, and Laos. The Cambodian government estimates that four to six million land mines, bombs, shells, and grenades still litter the countryside in that country from decades of conflict and genocide.

Some governments have active mine-clearing programs. People with mine detectors can find them, as can dogs trained to sniff out odors of explosive materials. When experts find a mine, they can defuse or explode it without hurting anyone. But the job is extremely dangerous and expensive. Many nations do not have the resources to clear land mines. The harm to people can be devastating. For example, in 2016 (the latest year for which complete figures are available), land mines killed or injured a reported 8,605 people in various countries around the world. Most of the victims were civilians, and nearly half of them were children.

Enter the Gambian pouched rat. These rats—as big as cats— have an excellent sense of smell and can learn to detect land mines. Cambodia, for example, has a land-mine clearing program that relies on the rats to locate buried land mines. The rats have found hundreds of unexploded land mines there since 2015. To do the work, a handler—walking on a path known to be free of mines—holds a leash attached to the rat's harness. The animal darts from side to side along the path, sniffing to detect the characteristic smell of land mines. A human with a land-mine detector machine would require two to three days to cover the same amount of terrain that a Gambian pouched rat can explore in thirty minutes.

The Cambodian Mine Action Centre trains Gambian pouched rats such as this one to clear mines. When they are only four weeks old, the rats begin training on inactive land mine fields. Cambodia is still littered with land mines after decades of war. Cambodia has one of the world's highest disability rates from land mine accidents.

Cambodian land mine clearing coordinator Theap Bunthourn explained the advantages of working with Gambian pouched rats, "They're cost efficient, they're easy to transport, they're easy to train, and they don't set off the mines because they're too light." When the rats find an unexploded land mine, they stick their noses up in the air and scratch the ground to alert the handler. After a rat finds a mine, it receives a piece of banana as a reward. The handler marks the spot, and bomb-disposal experts return later to detonate the explosive. The rats are easier to work with than dogs. They don't have the same need to bond with humans as dogs do. In fact, they don't bond with humans at all and will work with anyone.

DOLPHINS AND SEA LIONS JOIN THE NAVY

Beginning in 1960, the US Navy began to study dolphins and sea lions through its US Navy Mammal Marine Program (NMMP). To improve the design of torpedoes and submarines, military researchers wanted to understand more about how the marine mammals made their way in the ocean so quickly. It soon became apparent the animals had a range of very desirable abilities and skills beyond the torpedolike shape of their bodies that allows them to glide effortlessly through the water. For example, they can dive much deeper than people can and stay there for ten minutes without any harmful side effects. Dolphins also can locate objects easily with echolocation—their form of sonar. Sea lions have excellent vision and are especially good at spotting lost objects underwater. And both species are smart, friendly, and easily trained.

CETACEAN ECHOLOCATION

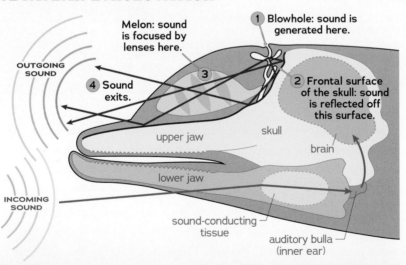

Melon: sound is focused by lenses here.

1 Blowhole: sound is generated here.

OUTGOING SOUND

4 Sound exits.

3

2 Frontal surface of the skull: sound is reflected off this surface.

upper jaw

skull

brain

lower jaw

INCOMING SOUND

sound-conducting tissue

auditory bulla (inner ear)

For a mammal to hear, sound must travel to a part of the ear called the inner, or middle, ear. Cetaceans (the order to which dolphins, whales, and porpoises belong) rely on echolocation as a way of hearing where an object is. They can find an object as small as a Ping-Pong ball as far away as 300 feet (91 m).

TRAINING DOLPHINS

Dolphins are extremely intelligent animals that are relatively easy to train because they're friendly and like people. Positive reinforcement is the most important aspect of training any animal whether it's a dolphin or a dog. Rewarding an animal for performing a desired behavior makes the animal want to perform the behavior correctly on command. The reward is usually food, toys, or affection from the trainer. Trainers don't punish animals for incorrect behavior. Instead, the trainer withholds the food treat and ignores the animal.

Trainers break down a desired behavior into a series of steps and then reward the animal for completing each step. For example, suppose the trainer wants to teach a dolphin to jump through a hoop. First, the trainer rewards the dolphin when it swims through the hoop in the water. Next, the hoop is raised partially out of the water. More rewards. Next, the hoop is held well above the water and the dolphin must jump through it to receive the reward.

Trainers use hand signals or voice commands as they work with the dolphins to tell the dolphin what behavior the trainer wants it to do. The trainer may use a whistle to signal the dolphin that it successfully completed the behavior and to return

Maintenance technician Christopher Burgess works with a bottlenose dolphin at Point Loma, California, before a night training exercise. The dolphins are trained to locate and mark mines in the ocean.

for a treat. Divers go underwater with dolphins to show them how to find a mine or to identify a stranger. After a dolphin has completed a complex task, it is rewarded—much as a dolphin that jumps through a hoop at SeaWorld would be.

Beginning in the 1960s, the militaries of both the United States and the Soviet Union used several species of dolphins to locate underwater mines and guard naval installations. The Soviet navy reportedly used dolphins to place mines on enemy ships and attach lethal devices to enemy divers. The US Navy publicly denied having a similar program. Richard L. Trout, a civilian animal trainer who worked for the US Navy, spoke to a *New York Times* journalist in 1990 and challenged the navy's public denial. "We were training dolphins and sea lions specifically for swimmer nullification," he said. "They were learning to kill enemy divers."

To nullify—kill or disable—a swimmer, trainers would attach a device to a dolphin's snout. When the animal was close to the target diver, it would jam the device into the swimmer and the device would discharge a .45 caliber bullet, seriously injuring or killing the person. Trout noted that the dolphins didn't do very well in the underwater training, partly because they are very friendly toward humans. Trout explained that during training, "when they were supposed to ram us with the guns, they either swam away or put their snouts on our shoulders, very affectionately. They were the worst at taking orders." However, in the twenty-first century, the US Navy did use dolphins to detect mines in the Persian Gulf during the Iraq War.

The mammal program, based in San Diego, trains bottlenose dolphins and California sea lions to find and retrieve equipment lost at sea. The animals also learn how to survey underwater sites with cameras attached to their fins. And they are able to find human enemies underwater. For example, *National Geographic* reported on a 2011 demonstration in San Diego, in which a former Navy SEAL's goal was to infiltrate the harbor. Handlers deployed dolphins and sea lions to patrol the area, and they caught the "enemy" SEAL every time. The sea lion even attached a clamp to the diver's leg allowing handlers on the surface to reel in the human SEAL as if he were a big fish!

ANIMAL RIGHTS

Many animal rights activists and ordinary citizens strongly object to using intelligent marine mammals for potentially dangerous military work. In response, the navy released a statement in 2012 saying, "During several decades of training and testing with explosives, only four marine mammals are known to have died during one training accident. Following this incident . . . we ceased all similar training." However, the navy does continue to train marine mammals to detect unarmed mines. For example, in the spring of 2017, the military newsletter *Task & Purpose* featured an article about navy dolphins sweeping the ocean floor near Key West, Florida, in a training exercise with unarmed mines. When the dolphins locate a bogus mine, they drop transponders near it. The devices then send radio signals to naval computers on land to locate the mine. If it were a live mine, ships can then avoid the site or could send divers to disable it.

The animals' living conditions with the naval program have come under fire. In April 2017, the San Diego CBS television station investigated the living conditions of dolphins with the mammal program. An animal rights activist spent months shooting video of the animals and then shared it with the TV station. The video showed the mammal program's eighty-five bottlenose dolphins confined in rows of pens 30 by 30 by 12 feet (9 by 9 by 3.6 m). Some of the animals were clearly in medical distress. The video showed one dolphin force-fed by staffers and another receiving intravenous fluid. "I've got videotape of animals literally for hours floating around in those pens supported by flotation [devices], not moving," said Russ Rector, a civilian dolphin trainer who studied the videos for the TV station. "That's not living. That's dying."

Soon after the TV station released the videos, the navy took down the mammal program's website. The navy ignored repeated requests from CBS News for more information about the program and for an on-camera interview. Instead, the navy released a report describing how

EAGLES BATTLE DRONES

People have trained falcons, hawks, and eagles for hundreds of years. Usually the predatory birds learned to hunt for game, such as rabbits, doves, and pheasants, for their owners. But France has a new use for them: the country is using eagles to take down drones. Four eagles—named Athos, Porthos, Aramis, and d'Artagnan after the literary Musketeers—destroy drones on command. The French military came up with the idea in 2015 after unidentified drones flew over the French presidential palace in Paris as well as over a restricted military site. No one was hurt. But later that year, after a terrorist attack in Paris, the French realized citizens could be vulnerable to drone attack.

So the military developed a plan to train eagles to take down drones. First, they hatched four eagle eggs atop drones so the birds would not fear the flying machines. The chicks chased the drones through grass on the ground and ate meat off them. An unnamed military source told a British newspaper that "we taught them to feed off the 'carcasses' of the drones. Now, when they see one of these craft, they think it has food coming off it and they intercept it. We're teaching them not just to attack [drones] but to detect them."

A French soldier trains an eagle during a military exercise at the Mont-de-Marsan Air Base in southwestern France. As drones are becoming more of a security threat, the French army is exploring new options for defense. They train royal eagles to chase down drones. The training program lasts six months.

By 2017 the eagles had been successfully trained to slam into drones and dive back to the ground with the wreckage clamped in their powerful talons. This does not harm the eagles. The birds are so successful at their task that the French military is planning for a second brood of eaglets. The military is also designing mittens of leather and Kevlar (an antiblast material) for the eagles to protect their talons if a drone explodes.

its dolphins had recently cleared training mines near San Clemente, Seal Beach, and San Diego Harbors. The navy said the exercises were critical to warfare readiness. Some people wonder if there is a better way for the navy to accomplish its work than by exploiting marine mammals. Navy media spokesperson James Fallin said, "While the long term goal remains to replace dolphins with machines, we are not there yet."

Many people, including scientists, are certain that animals are intelligent beings that feel pain and anxiety, love and loneliness, and a deep sense of loyalty to one another and to humans. If animals demonstrate so many traits to which humans can relate, don't they deserve to be treated with equal respect? Or are animals somehow lesser creatures to be treated differently than humans?

Nineteenth-century English philosopher and social reformer Jeremy Bentham said that when deciding on a being's rights, "The question is not 'Can they reason?' nor 'Can they talk?' but 'Can they suffer?'" Animals suffer in much the same way that people do, clearly feeling both physical and mental pain. How do we acknowledge and respect that suffering? Do we ignore it if it means that animal suffering saves human lives?

These are difficult questions to resolve. The US military has made improvements in the way it treats working animals. And as technology continues to develop, animals may no longer be asked to risk their lives to save ours. Until then, taking good care of the animals that do go to war with us is vital. In the words of Albert Schweitzer, a German philosopher and recipient of the 1952 Nobel Peace Prize, "Until he extends the circle of his compassion to all living things, man will not himself find peace."

SOURCE NOTES

6   Jilly Cooper, in Juliet Gardiner, *The Animals' War* (London: Piatkus Books/Imperial War Museum, 2006), 7.

7   Unnamed survivor, in Robert Weintraub, *No Better Friend: One Man, One Dog, and Their Extraordinary Story of Courage and Survival in WWII* (New York: Little Brown, 2015), 230.

8   Charles Jeffery, in Weintraub, *No Better Friend: One Man*, 15–16.

11 Frank Williams, in Weintraub, *No Better Friend: One Man*, 236.

12 "Hero Dog Theo Receives Animals' Victoria Cross," UK Ministry of Defense, October 25, 2012, https://www.gov.uk/government/news/hero -dog-theo-receives-animals-victoria-cross.

12 Weintraub. *No Better Friend: One Man*, 311.

13 Headline from a 1946 newspaper, in Robert Weintraub, *No Better Friend: A Man, a Dog, and Their Incredible True Story of Friendship and Survival in WWII*, YA version (New York: Little Brown, 2016), 238.

13 Frank Williams, in Weintraub, *No Better Friend: One Man*, 311.

14 John M. Kistler, *War Elephants* (Lincoln: University of Nebraska Press, 2007), 5–6.

15 Richard Lair, in Eric Scigliano, *Love, War and Circuses: The Age Old Relationship between Elephants and Humans* (New York, Houghton Mifflin Harcourt, 2002), 117.

15 Richard Lair, paraphrased in blog interview, *Julie Frick Travel Blog*, January 18, 2014, http://juliefrick.com/travels/2014/01/more-elephant -facts-meeting-with-imminent-elephant-biologist-richard-lair/.

15 Kistler, *War Elephants*, 5–6.

16 J. H. Williams, paraphrased in Simon Worrall, "How Burmese Elephants Helped Defeat the Japanese in World War II," *National Geographic*, September 27, 2014, https://news.nationalgeographic .com/news/2014/09/140928-burma-elephant-teak-kipling-japan -world-war-ngbooktalk/.

17 Po Toke, in J. H. Williams, *Elephant Bill* (New York: Doubleday, 1950), 215–216.

18 Williams, *Elephant Bill*, 218.

18 Ibid.

18 Ibid., 219.

19 Kistler, *War Elephants*, 3.

20 Williams, *Elephant Bill*, 67–68.

22   Alexander the Great, quoted in Kistler, *War Elephants*, 32, from Percy Sykes, *A History of Persia*, 1951.

23–24   Quintus Curtius Rufus, quoted in Kistler, *War Elephants*, 35.

24   Plutarch, quoted in Kistler, *War Elephants*, 36.

29   William Slim, in introduction, Williams, *Elephant Bill*.

30   Unnamed World War I soldier, quoted in "Michael Morpurgo on Horses' Military Service," *CBS News*, June 4, 2012, http://www.cbsnews.com/news/michael-morpurgo-on-horses-military-service/.

30   Donald L. Wasson, "Bucephalus." *Ancient History Encyclopedia*, last modified October 6, 2011, http://www.ancient.eu/Bucephalus/.

30   Ibid.

33   George Washington, letter to Congress, quoted in Donald N. Moran, "The Birth of the American Cavalry," *Liberty Tree Newsletter*, January 2008, available online at Revolutionary American War Archives, http://www.revolutionarywararchives.org/cavalry.html.

35   William Sherman, quoted in Deborah Grace, "The Horse in the Civil War," Reilly's Battery, July 2000 newsletter, http://www.reillysbattery.org/index.html.

36   Sydney Smith, quoted in Gardiner, *The Animals' War*, 40.

37   "An Impression from the Western Front," *Royal Society for the Prevention of Cruelty to Animals*, in Gardiner, *The Animals' War*, 37.

38   Michael Morpurgo, in "Michael Morpurgo on Horses' Military Service," *CBS News*.

41   George S. Patton, in Karen Jensen, "How General Patton and Some Unlikely Allies Saved the Prized Lipizzaner Stallions," *History Net*, September 18, 2009, http://www.historynet.com/patton-rescues-the-lipizzaner-stallions.htm.

41   Charles Reed, quoted in Jensen, "General Patton."

43   David Dempscy, quoted in Robin Hutton, *Sgt. Reckless: America's War Horse* (Washington DC: Regenery History, 2015), 53.

44   Harold Wadley, in Hutton, *Sgt. Reckless*, 89.

44   Randolph McCall Pate, in Hutton, *Sgt. Reckless*, 114–115.

45   Rafael Laskowski, in Lauren Cook, "NYPD Mounted Unit: Meet the Horses That Patrol NYC's Streets," *amNew York*, September 16, 2016, http://www.amny.com/news/nypd-mounted-unit-meet-the-horses-that-patrol-nyc-s-streets-1.12327370.

46   R. J. Cox, quoted in Jilly Cooper, *Animals in War*, 127–128.

47   Dave Babb, "History of the Mule," American Mule Museum, accessed July 7, 2017, http://www.mulemuseum.org/history-of-the-mule.html.

47   Charles Darwin, *What Mr. Darwin Saw in His Voyage Round the World in the Ship "Beagle"* (New York: Harper & Brothers, 1879), 33.

51   Cooper, *Animals in War*, 140.

54   Gardiner, *The Animals' War*, 60.

54   Cooper, *Animals in War*, 123.

58   John Fowler, in Wendell Mitchel Levi, *The Pigeon* (London: Wendell Levi, 1981), 7.

62   Robert Laplander, *Finding the Lost Battalion: Beyond the Rumors, Myths, and Legions of America's Famous WWI Epic* (Waterford, WI: A.E.F. Services/Lulu, 2017), 414.

62   Ibid.

62   Ibid., 444.

62   Fred Evermann, quoted in Laplander, *Finding the Lost Battalion*, 353–354.

62–63 J. L. Carney, quoted in "They Winged Their Way through Skies of Steel," *American Legion Weekly* 1, no. 9 (1919): 30.

65   "Winkie—the Bravest RAF Messenger Pigeon in WW2," Look and Learn History Picture Library, March 15, 2013, http://www.lookandlearn .com/blog/22580/winkie-the-bravest-raf-messenger-pigeon-in-ww2/.

66–67 Elaine Pendlebury, in Christopher Sleight, "The Pigeon That Saved a World War II Bomber Crew," *BBC News*, February 23, 2012, http://www.bbc.com/news/uk-scotland-tayside-central-17138990.

68–69 Tim Guilford, in Caroline Davies, "How Do Homing Pigeons Navigate? They Follow Roads," *Telegraph* (London), February 5, 2004, http:// www.telegraph.co.uk/news/uknews/1453494/How-do-homing-pigeons -navigate-They-follow-roads.html.

72   Jonathan Hagstrum, "Birds May Use Sound Maps to Navigate Huge Distances," *NPR*, February 1, 2013, http://www.npr.org/2013/02/01 /170884694/birds-may-use-sound-maps-to-navigate-huge-distances.

73   Mark Adam, in Kris Millgate, "Airports Recruiting Falcons to Keep Runways Safe," *Field & Stream*, June 24, 2016, http://www .fieldandstream.com/blogs/field-notes/airports-recruiting-falcons -to-keep-runways-safe.

74   Dwight D. Eisenhower, quoted in Cooper, *Animals in War*, 171.

74   Brian Hare and Vanessa Woods, in "We Didn't Domesticate Dogs. They Domesticated Us," *National Geographic,* March 13, 2013, http://news .nationalgeographic.com/news/2013/03/130302-dog-domestic-evolution -science-wolf-wolves-human/.

75   James Walker, in Peter Tyson, "Dogs' Dazzling Sense of Smell," *PBS NOVA*, October 4, 2012, http://www.pbs.org/wgbh/nova/nature/dogs-sense-of-smell.html.

78   Lisa Rogak, *The Dogs of War: The Courage, Love, and Loyalty of Military Working Dogs* (New York: Thomas Dunne Books, 2011), 60.

78   "Dogs and National Defense (Part 2) WWII & Korea War Dog History," United States War Dogs Association, accessed May 7, 2016, http://www.uswardogs.org/id25.html.

79   John Burnam, *A Soldier's Best Friend: Scout Dogs and Their Handlers in the Vietnam War* (New York: Union Square, 2008), 169.

79   John Burnam, in "John Burnam and Clipper," YouTube video, 12:29, posted by John Burnam, March 14, 2013, https://www.youtube.com/watch?v=qyDUBpPKkzU.

81   Burnam, *A Soldier's Best Friend*, 144.

81   Ibid., 243.

81–82   John Burnam, interviews with the author, August 26, 2015 September 20, 2015.

82   Ron Aiello, in Lisa Hoffman, "Seeking to Honor America's Four-Footed Soldiers, Vietnam Dog Handler Association," Memorial Day 2002, http://www.vdha.us/content230.html.

85   Kent Ferrell, in *Glory Hounds*, YouTube video, 1:24:05, posted by "K9kazooie," January 13, 2014, https://www.youtube.com/watch?v=iM5oSvXAUBI.

85   Brandon Liebert, in Maria Goodavage, *Soldier Dogs* (New York: Dutton, 2012), 33.

86   Charles Ogin, interview with the author, March 12, 2017.

86   Ibid.

86   Charles Ogin, in Anna Pongo, "Military Working Dog, Human Handler Bond in Baghdad," Department of Defense, February 28, 2017, https://www.defense.gov/News/Article/Article/1097173/military-working-dog-human-handler-bond-in-baghdad/.

86   Ogin, interview.

86   Stewart Hilliard, interview with the author, November 23, 2015.

87   Critics consensus, *Megan Leavey*, *Rotten Tomatoes*, accessed December 30, 2017, https://www.rottentomatoes.com/m/megan_leavey/.

87   Megan Leavey, in James O'Rourke, "Ex-Marine Hopes to Adopt the Canine Partner She Served With," *USA Today*, March 11, 2012, http://usatoday30.usatoday.com/news/nation/story/2012-03-09/marine-military-service-dog-reunite/53431138/1.

87   Michelle S. Brinn, "Former Pendleton Marine Reunited with Military Working Dog," Marines, April 9, 2012, http://www.pendleton.marines .mil/News/News-Article-Display/Article/537533/former-pendleton -marine-reunites-with-military-working-dog/.

87   Megan Leavey, in "Beloved Bomb-Sniffing Dog Who Retired to Live with Marine Handler Dies," *CBS News*, December 27, 2012, http://newyork .cbslocal.com/2012/12/27/beloved-bomb-sniffing-dog-who-retired-to-live -with-marine-handler-dies/.

88–89   Hilliard, interview.

90   Bruce Brickleff, in Nicholas Farina, "Canine Hoist Training," DVIDS, August 1, 2017, https://www.dvidshub.net/news/244132/canine-hoist -training?sub_id=40324&utm_campaign=subscriptions&utm _medium=email&utm_source=40324&utm_content=asset_link.

90   Angela Lowe, interview with the author, September 28, 2015.

91   Ibid.

91   Ibid.

92   David McLain, in "Our Story: The Chippewa Valley and Beyond," *Eau Claire (WI) Leader Telegram* special publication, 1976, accessed December 30, 2017, http://www.usgennet.org/usa/wi/county/eauclaire /history/ourstory/vol5/wareagle.html.

94   P. J. Hawthorne, *The Animal Victoria Cross—the Dickin Medal* (Barnsley, UK: Pen and Sword Military, 2012), 9.

96   Wojciech Narebski, in Alex Lockie, "The Story of Wojtek: The 440-Pound Bear That Drank, Smoked, and Carried Weapons for the Polish Army during World War II," *Business Insider*, September 23, 2016, http:// www.businessinsider.com/polish-army-bear-wojtek-world-war-ii-2016 -9/#after-being-released-from-a-siberian-labor-camp-during-the-nazi -invasion-of-russia-in-1942-the-22nd-polish-supply-brigade-began-a-long -trek-south-toward-persia-along-the-way-they-bought-an-orphaned-bear-1.

98   Max Knoblauch, "U.S. Marine Corps Bulldog Chesty Gets Promoted to Corporal, Is Good Boy," *Mashable*, August 30, 2014, http://mashable.com/ 2014/08/30/marine-corps-chesty-bulldog-promoted/#_6_nMi9CKsq9.

101   William Blandy, in Jonathan M. Weisgall, *Operation Crossroads: The Atomic Tests at Bikini Atoll* (Annapolis, MD: Naval Institute, 1994), 120.

102   Joint Task Force press release #48 DOECIC 100995, 1945, quoted in Weisgall, *Operation Crossroads*, 120.

102   "Animals Used in Bikini A-bomb Test Reported to Be 'Dying like Flies,'" *Los Angeles Times*, July 15, 1946.

103   J. W. August and Mari Payton, "Marines Speak Out about Using Live Animals in Trauma Training," *NBC News*, February 8, 2017,

https://www.nbcsandiego.com/news/local/Marines-Speak-Out-About
-Using-Live-Animals-in-Trauma-Training-413103143.html.

104   Cooper, *Animals in War*, 211.

105   Emily Pieracci, DVM, interview with the author, September 17, 2015.

105   Burnam, interview.

106   Bill Childress, in Rebecca Frankel, "Actually, No, There Are No
Military Dogs Left Behind," *Foreign Policy*, September 19, 2014, http://
foreignpolicy.com/2014/09/19/wdotw-actually-no-there-are-no-military
-dogs-left-behind/.

106–107   Dustin Weeks, interview with the author, November 18, 2015.

107   Ibid.

107   Karl Stefanowicz, interviews with the author, August–September 2015.

107   Ibid.

108   Jan McLoughlin, in Erika Ritchie, "Camp Pendleton War Dog Loses
Leg in Bomb Blast, Gets Highest Military Honor," *Orange County (CA)
Register*, April 28, 2016, http://www.ocregister.com/articles/lucca-713832
-willingham-dog.html.

109   Rebecca Frankel, in Thomas E. Ricks, "Rebecca's War Dog of the Year:
I'm Off to Phoenix Next Week to Adopt Dyngo," *Foreign Policy*, May 6,
2016, http://foreignpolicy.com/2016/05/06/rebeccas-war-dog-of-the-year
-im-off-to-phoenix-next-week-to-adopt-dyngo/.

109   Rebecca Frankel, interview with the author, August 28, 2017.

109   Ibid.

111   Theap Bunthourn, in Michael Sullivan. "In Cambodia, Rats Are Being
Trained to Sniff Out Land Mines and Save Lives," *NPR*, July 31,
2015, http://www.npr.org/sections/parallels/2015/07/31/427112786
/in-cambodia-rats-are-being-trained-to-sniff-out-land-mines-and
-save-lives.

114   Richard L. Trout, in "Navy Suspends a Plan to Use Dolphins as Guards,"
New York Times, July 24, 1990, http://www.nytimes.com/1990/07/24/us
/navy-suspends-a-plan-to-use-dolphins-as-guards.html.

114   Ibid.

115   Shawn Eklund, "Just the Facts: Navy Training and Marine Mammals,"
Navy/Department of Defense, July 13, 2012, http://navylive.dodlive
.mil/2012/07/13/just-the-facts-navy-training-and-marine-mammals/.

115   Russ Rector, in David Gotfredson, "Grayfish: Video Exposes Navy
Dolphin Care on San Diego Bay," *CBS 8 News*, April 27, 2017, http://
www.cbs8.com/story/35271969/grayfish-video-exposes-navy-dolphin
-care-on-san-diego-bay.

116   Unnamed military source, in David Burke, "French Police Training EAGLES to Attack Drones over Fears ISIS Could Use the Gadgets to Carry Out Terror Attacks," *Daily Mail* (London), February 20, 2017, http://www.dailymail.co.uk/news/article-4241632/French-police -training-EAGLES-attack-drones.html.

117   James Fallin, in Gotfredson, "Grayfish."

117   Jeremy Bentham, PETA, accessed August 17, 2017, https://www.peta .org/about-peta/why-peta/why-animal-rights/.

117   Albert Schweitzer, *Kulturphilosophie* (Biederstein, Munchen, 1923).

GLOSSARY

deployment: the movement of troops to a place or position for military action

Dickin Medal: a British animal award that goes to animals for bravery while serving during military conflict. Winners have included pigeons, dogs, horses, and one cat. The Dickin Medal is the most prestigious award an animal can receive and is awarded by the People's Dispensary for Sick Animals, a British veterinary charity.

drone: a pilotless radio-controlled aircraft used for recreation, aerial reconnaissance, or bombing

echolocation: the ability of animals such as dolphins and bats to emit high-pitched sounds whose wavelengths reflect off an object or creature and return to the animal. The animal uses the returning wavelengths to determine where the object is and its size. These clues may help the animal recognize the object.

Gambian pouched rat: a large African rodent that can be trained to detect buried land mines in former war zones

gunboat: a small, well-armed vessel designed for rivers and shallow water

handler: the person who trains or works with an animal such as a military working dog or a dolphin

improvised explosive device (IED): an explosive device made from easily available materials for injuring or killing others. Enemy forces may hide IEDs in abandoned buildings, cars, and homes or bury them in roads and ditches. Triggered remotely or when a person (or dog) comes in contact with the IED, the devices cause severe injury and even death.

insurgent: a person who revolts against civil authority or an established government. The term also refers to people independently fighting US forces and their allies in the Middle East in the twenty-first century.

land mine: an explosive device laid on or just under the surface of the ground to injure or kill people

mahout: a person who helps train elephants and who rides and cares for them

military working dog (MWD): a specially trained dog, owned by the US military, that works with a handler to perform duties such as detecting bombs or drugs and chasing, catching, and detaining intruders and suspects. The dogs also patrol bases and military camps and provide protection for high-profile political leaders and other public figures.

prisoner of war (POW): a person captured by the opposing side during a time of war. The term usually refers to members of the military.

quarantine: a period or place of isolation for animals that have arrived from a foreign land or been exposed to infectious or contagious disease to prevent the real or potential spread of disease

sonar: the method of echolocation that animals such as bats or dolphins use in air or water to locate objects

SELECTED BIBLIOGRAPHY

Burnam, John C. *A Soldier's Best Friend: Scout Dogs and Their Handlers in the Vietnam War.* New York: Sterling, 2008.

Cooper, Jilly. *Animals in War.* London: Corgi Books, 2000.

Gardiner, Juliet. *The Animals' War.* London: Piatkus Books/Imperial War Museum, 2006.

Gotfredson, David. "Grayfish: Video Exposes Navy Dolphin Care on San Diego Bay." *CBS 8 News*, April 27, 2017. http://www.cbs8.com/story/35271969 /grayfish-video-exposes-navy-dolphin-care-on-san-diego-bay.

Hagstrum, Jonathan. "Birds May Use Sound Maps to Navigate Huge Distances." *NPR*, February 1, 2013. http://www.npr.org/2013/02/01/170884694/birds-may -use-sound-maps-to-navigate-huge-distances.

Hare, Brian, and Vanessa Woods. "We Didn't Domesticate Dogs. They Domesticated Us." *National Geographic*, March 13, 2013. http://news.nationalgeographic.com /news/2013/03/130302-dog-domestic-evolution-science-wolf-wolves-human/.

Hutton, Robin. *Sgt. Reckless: America's War Horse.* Washington, DC: Regenery History, 2015.

Jensen, Karen. "How General Patton and Some Unlikely Allies Saved the Prized Lipizzaner Stallions." *History Net*, September 18, 2009. http://www.historynet .com/patton-rescues-the-lipizzaner-stallions.htm.

Kistler, John M. *War Elephants.* Lincoln: University of Nebraska Press, 2007.

Levi, Wendell Mitchel. *The Pigeon.* London: Wendell Levi, 1981.

Martinic, G. "Military Live Tissue Trauma Training Using Animals in the U.S.—Its Purpose, Importance and Commentary on Military Medical Research and the Debate on Use of Animals in Military Training." *Journal of Military and Veterans' Health* 20, no. 4 (November 2012): 5. http://jmvh.org/wp-content/uploads /2012/11/JMVH-November-2012_print.pdf.

Scigliano, Eric. *Love, War and Circuses: The Age Old Relationship between Elephants and Humans.* New York: Houghton Mifflin Harcourt, 2002.

Selk, Avi. "Terrorists Are Building Drones. France Is Destroying Them with Eagles." *Washington Post*, February 21, 2017. http://www.washingtonpost.com/news /worldviews/wp/2017/02/21/terrorists-are-building-drones-france-is-destroying -them-with-eagles/?utm_term=.9ab2c9b8c03a.

Sullivan, Michael. "In Cambodia, Rats Are Being Trained to Sniff Out Land Mines and Save Lives." *NPR*, July 31, 2015. http://www.npr.org/sections /parallels/2015/07/31/427112786/in-cambodia-rats-are-being-trained-to-sniff -out-land-mines-and-save-lives.

Teichner, Martha. "Michael Morpurgo on Horses' Military Service." *CBS News*, June 4, 2012. http://www.cbsnews.com/news/michael-morpurgo-on-horses -military-service/.

Tyson, Peter. "Dogs' Dazzling Sense of Smell." *PBS NOVA*, October 4, 2012. http:// www.pbs.org/wgbh/nova/nature/dogs-sense-of-smell.html.

Wasson, Donald L. "Bucephalus." *Ancient History Encyclopedia*. Last modified October 6, 2011. http://www.ancient.eu/Bucephalus/.

Williams, J. H. *Elephant Bill*. New York: Doubleday, 1950.

FURTHER INFORMATION

Books

Frankel, Rebecca. *War Dogs: Tales of Canine Heroism, History, and Love*. New York: St. Martin's, 2016. This young readers' version of the author's well-known adult book by the same name explores how MWDs and their handlers work in the twenty-first-century military. She also discusses the rich history of the dog–military handler working relationship. The author has written about MWDs for international audiences since 2010.

Goldish, Meish. *Dolphins in the Navy*. New York: Bearport, 2012. This book describes how the US Navy trains dolphins to protect American sailors and ships from danger. Dolphins can find mines and locate enemy swimmers using their special senses in ways that people cannot.

Goldsmith, Connie. *Bombs over Bikini*. Minneapolis: Twenty-First Century Books, 2014. Learn about the US nuclear testing program in the Marshall Islands after World War II and how it changed the world forever. The United States detonated sixty-seven nuclear bombs between 1946 and 1958. The twelfth bomb became the world's first nuclear disaster as it sent radiation over inhabited atolls. The program also tested the effects of radiation on thousands of animals.

———. *Dogs at War: Military Canine Heroes*. Minneapolis: Twenty-First Century Books, 2017. Through numerous personal interviews, this book describes the selection and training of military working dogs. It also discusses the jobs they do in war and in peace in every branch of the US military.

Morpurgo, Michael. *War Horse*. London: HarperCollins UK, 2010. The military purchase Joey, a young horse in Great Britain, and ships him to France early in World War I. His owner, Albert, promises to get Joey back home to his country farm. The Germans capture Joey, and he works in the trenches of the western front. This popular novel has been turned into a movie and a play.

Weintraub, Robert. *No Better Friend: A Man, a Dog, and Their Incredible True Story of Friendship and Survival in World War I*. New York: Little Brown, 2016. This book tells the incredible and true story of Frank Williams (of Britain's Royal Air Force) and Judy, a purebred pointer. The two met as prisoners of war during World War II. Judy became the war's only official canine POW.

Websites and Organizations

Atlantic
https://www.theatlantic.com/photo/2014/04/world-war-i-in-photos-animals-at-war/507320/
This photo gallery of the *Atlantic* magazine website contains forty-five excellent and moving photos of animals in World War I, including dogs, pigeons, horses, camels, and an elephant.

BBC News
https://www.bbc.co.uk/newsbeat/article/35967137/see-some-of-the-67-animals-whove-been-handed-the-dickin-medal-for-bravery
At this site, visitors will find biographies of several of the animals that have received the prestigious Dickin Medal for bravery and service during wartime.

British Library—World War One
https://www.bl.uk/world-war-one/articles/animals-and-war
This article tells about the many animals used by military forces in World War I, including dogs, pigeons, horses, and mules.

International Campaign to Ban Landmines
http://www.icbl.org/en-gb/home.aspx
This international organization is a global network of nongovernmental organizations in about one hundred countries that works to clear land mines from countries so that people can move about their land without fearing for their lives. Launched in 1992, the organization not only tracks land mine injuries and deaths but also monitors progress of countries that have signed a treaty to stop land mine use.

National Marine Mammal Foundation (NMMF)
http://www.nmmf.org/
The foundation works to improve and protect life for marine mammals, people, and oceans. The group develops education programs, conducts research that benefits marine mammals, and supports the navy in the care and training of its marine mammals. It also works to improve the health of both captive and wild marine mammals.

National Pigeon Association
http://www.npausa.com/
Founded in 1920, the National Pigeon Association is an all-breeds pigeon club with an international membership. It promotes and educates pigeon fanciers around the world in the care of pigeons, including their feeding, housing, and training. It offers information on pigeon racing programs and details about the many kinds of pigeons.

People for the Ethical Treatment of Animals (PETA)
https://www.peta.org/issues/animals-used-for-experimentation/animals-used-experimentation-factsheets/military-war-animals/
Read the organization's philosophy of opposing the use of animals in war and for other military-related activities. PETA is the largest animal rights organization in the world with more than sixty-five million supporters.

Peoples Dispensary for Sick Animals
https://www.pdsa.org.uk/what-we-do/animal-honours/the-dickin-medal
Learn about all the animals—pigeons, dogs, horses, and a cat —that have received the Dickin Medal since the founding of the Peoples Dispensary for Sick Animals in 1943.

Top 10 Famous War Horses in History
  https://www.wonderslist.com/10-famous-war-horses-in-history/
  Learn about the most famous warhorses in history, including Alexander's
  Bucephalus and the US horse Reckless, one of the most famous warhorses of all.

United States War Dogs Association
  http://www.uswardogs.org/
  Maintained by Vietnam War veteran and MWD handler Ron Aiello, this
  site provides the history of US war dogs since World War I along with news,
  information about dog adoption and medical care, and the personal story of
  Aiello and his dog Stormy.

Movies and Videos

"French Army Grooms Eagles to Take Down Drones." YouTube video, 2:02. Posted
  by the AFP News Agency, February 23, 2017. https://www.youtube.com
  /watch?v=TseOHDBZ8MA. (French interviews have simultaneous voiceover
  English translation.) Faced with the risk of drones being used to snoop or carry
  out attacks on French soil, the French air force is training four golden eagles to
  take out unmanned aircraft in mid-flight.

Glory Hounds. YouTube video, 1:24:05. Posted by "k9kazooie," January 13, 2014.
  https://www.youtube.com/watch?v=iM5oSvXAUBI. Filmed in Afghanistan, this
  excellent documentary profiles four MWDs and their handlers in the war zone
  as they locate enemy insurgents and dangerous explosives.

"Homing Pigeons in France during WWI 1918." YouTube video, 9:52.
  Posted by OHSfilm, March 21, 2014. https://www.youtube.com
  /watch?v=k2A3GORFCPg. This silent video (sound wasn't yet part of video at
  the time) provides excellent footage of soldiers in World War I carrying pigeons
  to the front lines in baskets and pigeons getting messages and returning to
  their lofts.

"Military Dogs Trained and Bred in San Antonio." *KENS5 News* video, 3:23. Posted
  May 3, 2016. http://www.kens5.com/news/local/a-look-inside-jbsa-lacklands
  -military-%20working-dog-breeding-program/165397021. Watch puppy training
  at Lackland Air Force Base, where military personnel train American MWDs for
  work around the world.

"Mine Sniffing Rats of Africa." *New York Times* video, 2:56. 2015. https://www
  .nytimes.com/video/opinion/100000003635415/the-mine-sniffing-rats-of-africa
  .html. Take a firsthand look at the care and training of Gambian pouched rats
  as they sniff out land mines in Angola.

Miracle of the White Stallions. 1:58. Directed by Arthur Hiller. Burbank, CA: Walt
  Disney, 1963. This movie was developed from Alois Podhajsky's memoir, *My
  Dancing White Horses.* Podhajsky was an Austrian colonel who worked with
  General George Patton at the end of World War II to save the famous Lipizzaner
  stallions from the advancing Soviet Army.

"Simon the Cat." YouTube video, 1:14. Posted by scapa8, February 8, 2012. Filmmaker: ITN Adam Holloway. https://www.youtube.com/watch?v =iq7BMGbThHk. This brief film clip shows the British ship USS *Amethyst* returning to England with Simon the cat on board. It also contains one of the few videos of Simon.

"Sgt. Reckless: Korean War Horse Hero." YouTube video, 3:36. Posted by Robin Hutton, August 8, 2010. https://www.youtube.com/watch?v=YIo3ZfA9da0. Video clips and still photos describe Reckless and her achievements with the US Marine Corps in the Korean War.

"United States Navy Marine Mammal Program." YouTube video, 2:19. Posted by Wiz Science, August 7, 2015. https://www.youtube.com/watch?v=txCUFGCVWBg. This video briefly introduces the US Navy Marine Mammal Program, which trains dolphins and sea lions to detect mines and intercept enemy divers. The navy deleted its website about the program after negative publicity from an NBC television investigation in 2017.

War Horse. 2.26. Directed by Steven Spielberg. Burbank, CA: Touchstone Pictures, 2011. This movie is based on the novel of the same name by Michael Morpurgo. It tells the story of a British horse in World War I that was sold to the military. The horse, seized by the Germans, worked for both sides and returns home at the end of the war.

INDEX

PHOTO ACKNOWLEDGMENTS

Image credits: Backgrounds: FARBAI/Shutterstock.com; natrot/Shutterstock.com
Content: AP Photo/Press Association, pp. 2–3; Topical Press Agency/Hulton Archive/
Getty Images, p. 7; Jack Taylor/Getty Images, p. 12; geogphotos/Alamy Stock Photo,
p. 15; Universal History Archive/Getty Images, p. 23; Wikimedia Commons (public
domain), pp. 25, 48, 80; The Print Collector Heritage Images/Collection/Newscom,
p. 27; U.S. Army Photo, p. 28; Konstantinos Tsakalidis/Alamy Stock Photo, p. 31;
Jon Bower/LOOP IMAGES/Corbis Documentary/Getty Images, p. 33; Universal
History Archive/Getty Images, p. 34; DeAgostini/Getty Images, p. 37; Universal
Images Group/Getty Images, p. 39; PhotoQuest/Getty Images, p. 40; U.S. Army
Photo, p. 43; TIMOTHY A. CLARY/AFP/Getty Images, p. 45; United States
Military Academy Library, p. 47; Universal History Archive/UIG/Getty Images,
pp. 50, 52; Bettmann/Getty Images, p. 55; Jeremy Richards/Alamy Stock Photo, p. 56;
Thumbelina/Shutterstock.com, p. 59; adoc-photos/Getty Images, p. 61; Popperfoto/
Getty Images, p. 65; Laura Westlund/Independent Picture Service, pp. 69, 84, 112;
Yale Joel/Life Magazine/The LIFE Picture Collection/Getty Images, p. 71; Teri
Virbickis/Shutterstock.com, p. 73; U.S. Army Photo by Staff Sgt. Perry Aston, p. 75,
Universal History Archive/Getty Images, p. 77; courtesy of John Burnam, p. 79; U.S.
Army Photo by Staff Sgt. Stacy L. Pearsall, p. 83; © Matthew Mahon/Redux, p. 88;
US Air Force photo, p. 90; Keystone Pictures USA/Alamy Stock Photo, p. 93; Mark
Cuthbert/UK Press/Getty Images, p. 95; US Marines Photo/Alamy Stock Photo,
p. 98; Keystone/Getty Images, p. 101; US Air Force photo by U.S. Army Sgt. Jason
Brace, 86th Infantry Brigade Combat Team, Task Force Wolverine Public Affairs,
p. 105; © Dustin Weeks, p. 106; AP Photo/Press Association, p. 108; SAMRANG
PRING/REUTERS/Newscom, p. 111; Laura Westlund/Independent Picture Service,
p. 112; DoD photo by Lt. David Bennett/Released, p. 113; AFP / GEORGES
GOBET/Getty Images, p. 116.

Cover: Getty Images North America/Getty Images.

ABOUT THE AUTHOR

Connie Goldsmith has written twenty-two nonfiction books for middle grade and young adult readers and has also published more than two hundred magazine articles for adults and children. Her books include *Pandemic: How Climate, the Environment, and Superbugs Increase the Risk*; *Addiction and Overdose: Confronting an American Crisis*; *Dogs at War: Military Canine Heroes*; *Understanding Suicide: A National Epidemic*; *The Ebola Epidemic: The Fight, The Future* (a Junior Library Guild selection and *Kirkus* starred review); and *Bombs over Bikini*, a Junior Library Guild Selection, a Children's Book Committee at Bank Street College Best Children's Book of the Year, and an SCBWI Crystal Kite winner.

She is a member of the Society of Children's Book Writers and Illustrators and a member of the Authors Guild. Goldsmith is a registered nurse with a bachelor of science degree in nursing and a master of public administration degree in health care. When she's not writing, she visits with friends and family, pounds out the miles on her treadmill, plays with her crazy cats, and hikes along the American River near Sacramento, California, where she lives.